that cheese plate will

change your life

that cheese plate will change your life

creative gatherings and self-care
with the cheese by numbers method

Marissa Mullen

ILLUSTRATED BY SARA GILANCHI

THE DIAL PRESS · NEW YORK

Published in the United States by The Dial Press,
an imprint of Random House, a division of
Penguin Random House LLC, New York.

THE DIAL PRESS and the HOUSE colophon are registered
trademarks of Penguin Random House LLC.

Photographs on pages 2 and 286 © Nico Schinco

LIBRARY OF CONGRESS CATALOGING-IN-PUBLICATION DATA
NAMES: Mullen, Marissa, author.
TITLE: That cheese plate will change your life: creative gatherings and self-care
with the cheese by numbers method / Marissa Mullen.
DESCRIPTION: New York: The Dial Press, 2020. | Includes index.
IDENTIFIERS: LCCN 2019036418 (print) | LCCN 2019036419 (ebook) |
ISBN 9780593157596 (hardcover) | ISBN 9780593157602 (ebook)
SUBJECTS: LCSH: Cheese—Varieties. | Appetizers. |
Cooking (Cheese) | LCGFT: Cookbooks.
CLASSIFICATION: LCC TX382 .M85 2020 (print) |
LCC TX382 (ebook) | DDC 641.6/73—dc23

LC record available at https://lccn.loc.gov/2019036418

LC ebook record available at https://lccn.loc.gov/2019036419

Printed in China on acid-free paper

randomhousebooks.com

14

Illustrations by Sara Gilanchi

This book is dedicated to

Ellen and Jim Mullen,

who taught me the importance

of bringing together

the ones you love.

contents

contents

that cheese plate will
change your life

introduction

"That cheese plate will change your life."

Okay, okay, I can feel you rolling your eyes at me, thinking, "Well, that feels like a bit of an overstatement." And maybe it is. Or, maybe, there's some truth in this idea. Because here's what I believe: cheese plates are self-care.

These days, in our Instagram-laden world, *self-care* usually means applying a face mask, cutting out carbs, sipping green juice, or spending Friday night in a bathtub full of flower petals. It's usually tied to a feeling of restriction or a temporary fix. But let's be real: a sheet mask and green juice can only do so much. True self-care is something different, something deeper: we care for ourselves when we allow ourselves the time, energy, and space to practice or learn about—or indulge in—the things that we love most. These are the things that bring us joy and make us feel connected to our most authentic selves and to others. For me, that thing has always been cheese.

In college, my friends and I had frequent wine and cheese parties, attempting a stab at newfound adulthood. Our ancient Boston apartment lacked a living room, so the kitchen was the heart and soul of every gathering. Although we had limited funds, we found ways to come together over hunks of cheddar and some prepackaged meat. I discovered that crafting these cheese plates for my friends was a great way for me to get creative while trying new and interesting flavors. Similarly, photography was another artistic hobby of mine, and I began to learn more about the world of social media as I earned a degree in music business and communications. As food accounts became a growing trend on Instagram, I decided to start my own account to showcase my creations, and @ThatCheesePlate was born. Over the years, this evolved into a monthly event called "the cheese party": I built elaborate cheese plates while everyone gathered in my tiny apartment, sharing stories and catching up. The cheese plate was always the most popular guest at the party.

Then I got my dream job in the music industry, which meant countless late nights and weekend travel. Limited free time was my norm. When I did have time off, making a cheese plate was my relaxing activity of choice. It was always so satisfying to see a design come together out of wedges of cheese, slices of salami, and the colorful produce I'd find at my local market. I learned that the simple act of slicing cheese could be meditative. I found a sacred space in the kitchen of my humble Brooklyn apartment. Full of natural light, it became my sanctuary after a long workweek. I loved to spend Saturday afternoons decompressing while I arranged and photographed my cheese plate creations. There's something cathartic in creating an intricate and beautiful plate, which my friends and I in turn would completely devour.

As my plates became more elaborate, I realized how much time the building process could take. You need to prep the cheese, fold the salami, and deliberately cut the produce. Taking the time to follow these steps forced me to slow down, a welcome change from how I spent the weeks at my day job. Every time, I was instinctively following a step-by-step process, filling in elements by sections. I asked my friend Sara Gilanchi, a talented illustrator, to sketch one of my plates numbering the illustration with *1* as Cheese, *2* as Meat, *3* as Produce, *4* as Crunch, *5* as Dip, and *6* as Garnish. Thus, the Cheese By Numbers method was born.

This process was deceptively easy, yet sticking to it elevated my plates to a new level. I decided to launch a second account on Instagram called @CheeseByNumbers to document this method in further detail. I'd photograph and post each step in the process, starting with the cheese arranged on the plate, followed by the Salami River (more on that later!), and so on. This process really resonated with people. Creating a cheese plate seems intimidating at first, but Cheese By Numbers makes the building process simple and accessible. This account started to shift into something bigger than I anticipated.

Over the next few months, I felt the increased momentum of what I had built. I balanced television appearances, press inquiries, and food events with my already-demanding job in the entertainment industry. Simultaneously I launched That Cheese Class, a "build your own cheese plate" workshop. The Cheese By Numbers method encouraged the class members to get creative and break outside their comfort zone. I really loved my job working in music, but I started to feel as if my heart really belonged to what had just been my side-hustle: cheese. Building plates and teaching workshops made me feel both creative and grounded—two feelings I hadn't experienced in a long time. I started to wonder, What if I could do this full time? I decided to take a leap and quit my day job. And that's when it hit me: That Cheese Plate changed my life.

I wrote this book as a template and a guide, but feel free to get creative and substitute items that work for you. We will start with the basics and will then journey through the Cheese By Number method, starting with cheese, followed by meat, produce, crunch, dip, and garnish. In each chapter we will dive deeper into these six steps, introducing Cheese By Number maps and a variety of simple recipes to elevate your plate. My hope is that you can feel a sense of ease by taking the guesswork out of a timeless appetizer. You don't need to be a professional food stylist or chef to make a cheese plate—you can easily create something beautiful to impress your guests and yourself!

So take your passion and run with it. Do what inspires you. Growth takes time, and the process is the most important part. Hopefully this book will help you slow down a bit, appreciate what's around you, get motivated, and make That Cheese Plate.

the cheese by numbers method

The Cheese By Numbers method is a simple, mindful way to guarantee a beautiful plate every time. However, it's much more than just a recipe for a stunning cheese plate. By following each step in the process, you'll learn more about the individual ingredients and how together they make a balanced plate. Remember these steps below, and repeat them like a mantra:

1—CHEESE
2—MEAT
3—PRODUCE
4—CRUNCH
5—DIP
6—GARNISH

Each Cheese By Numbers map in this book includes a key, which will be your grocery list. The key is organized according to the Cheese By Numbers method, and each ingredient is listed in clockwise order, starting at the top of the plate. But remember, the most important thing is to be creative. You do you. If a plate calls for cheddar but you're not really a fan, switch it out for something you do like! Along with the key, you'll see a foolproof step-by-step guide to building the plate. I'm here to make cheese plates easy, accessible, and fun—a source of relaxation, not stress.

preparation
is key

the mind and mood

Creating a cheese plate is all about getting back to the basics, grounding yourself, and expressing gratitude for your food and the company of the people who share it with you. It's important to be mindful and to open yourself up to the present moment while building a cheese plate. First, find a calm setting with space to prep all the deliciousness that will go on your plate. Give yourself enough time and settle into the process. Maybe put on a soothing playlist and jam out while you're slicing the cheese. Think of building a cheese plate like going to yoga class: you have to work to earn the Savasana, but the practice is a meditation in and of itself.

Building a cheese plate definitely doesn't need to be a solo activity. Sharing the joy of cheese with someone else is just as therapeutic—and two cheese lovers are always better than one. Figure out which steps in the process you each connect with and split up the duties. If folding salami is your thing, call dibs on the Salami River. If you'd rather chop fruits and veggies, prep the produce. It's a way for you to communicate with the people close to you and create something together.

You may have picked up this book and thought, "How can cheese plates be self-care? Cheese isn't even healthy?!" This, my friend, is a myth. Cheese is actually full of calcium and beneficial fatty acids, providing a great source of protein and nutrients. But if dairy doesn't float your boat, make a cheeseless cheese plate! There's more to it than just cheese, from rich green vegetables to protein-packed meat. Ask yourself, "What will make *me* feel good?" Practice the art of balance, but let yourself indulge when you want. Find your happy medium. The best part of the process is sharing your plate afterward. Dig into the different cheeses, create your own personal pairings, and enjoy the moment around you.

the foundation

Boards: Once you've settled into your meditative mood, find a flat surface to build upon. In addition to a dedicated cheese board, this could even be something as simple as a cutting board, a dinner plate, or even your kitchen counter.

Ramekins: Use ramekins to hold the dips and briny items on your cheese plate. Set them up on your board before you start to create your plate so that you have a foundation to build around. I typically put jam, honey, and compotes into 2-ounce glass ramekins and use slightly larger ramekins for briny items like olives and cornichons.

Prep: It always helps to precut your cheese, fold your meat, and prep your washed produce for easy assembly. You can do this ahead of time, even the day before! Having your workstation already set up makes the building process efficient and avoids any mess or scraps to deal with while constructing.

A Note on Serving Sizes: I decided to leave serving sizes out of the Cheese By Numbers maps. Consider the purpose of your cheese plate. Is it an appetizer before a big dinner? Is it the main meal? The rule of thumb is about 3 ounces of cheese per person, but I can easily eat more than that. Here's my estimate:

8″ plate: 2 to 4 people

10″ plate: 4 to 6 people

12″ plate: 6 to 8 people

15″ plate: 8 to 12 people

For more than 12 people, just keep restocking the board when it runs low, or check out my grazing table at the end of the book. That will feed 15 to 20 people for an appetizer.

that cracker plate

As essential to That Cheese Plate as a faithful sidekick, That Cracker Plate holds all of your extra crackers and bread so you can maximize space on your plate and still have enough carbs to go around. A dinner plate, baking dish, or tray all make perfect cracker plates. Some of my favorite crunch includes flatbread crackers, seeded crackers, French baguettes, focaccia, sourdough bread, water crackers, and butter crackers.

1

SAY
CHEESE

For me, cheese used to be a rare, fleeting, special occasion thing. Happily, it's become ordinary. By that, I mean it's a component of my everyday life, from kids' lunches to gathering with my friends. That's how it should be. This isn't fancy food— it's essential food, and it's a real way to connect with and support farmers all over the world.

—LIZ THORPE, CHEESE EXPERT AND
AUTHOR OF *THE BOOK OF CHEESE*

Step 1 of the Cheese By Numbers method is, of course, the cheese. Cheese ignites the senses. Feel the texture of cutting into a fresh wedge of goat cheese. Taste the complex notes in an aged Parmigiano-Reggiano. See the creamy interior of a dollop of burrata. Smell the pungent aroma of a blue cheese. Listen to the sound of bubbling baked brie fresh out of the oven. Let the cheese spark conversation between you and your loved ones. It's an all-around sensory experience.

When I started making my own plates, cheese also became my vehicle for expression and creativity. From its tasting notes—whether nutty, sharp, or buttery—to its range of shapes and textures, cheese gives us the chance to discover new flavors, and learn about different cultures. The versatility of cheese is limitless.

On That Cheese Plate, the cheese is the focus, the starting point in exploring our tastes and building on them in perfect harmony. From gruyère to cheddar and brie to blue, cheese provides a wide range of opportunity for flavor pairings and sets the tone for the rest of the plate. This chapter will help you choose your cheese with intention and give you a feel for the different varieties and styles (and most important, help you find what types of cheese you enjoy). Branch out, try something new, and submit to the cheesy goodness.

your go-to cheese guide

I never thought there could be too much of a good thing when it came to cheese, but then I stepped into my local cheese shop and saw how many options there were. Luckily, cheesemongers exist, and they have the answers to all of our questions. Almost everything I know about cheese came from befriending (read: relentlessly questioning) cheesemongers, and I've never looked back. Plus, I love that you can ask to try literally any cheese in a cheese shop. Trust me, it's a true-life hack. (Forget Disneyland, cheese shops are the happiest place on earth.) But even if you don't have access to a cheese shop, supermarkets have all kinds of great varieties, and if you're feeling ambitious, you can even track down harder-to-find cheeses online. I typically like to choose cheeses with different types of milk, textures, or flavors for each of my plates, so I've tried to keep the cheeses in this book diverse and interesting. But keep in mind that they're all suggestions, so if something doesn't line up with your price point or you can't find it at your local store, there are always substitutions you can make. Here's a basic guide to get you started.

cheese textures

FRESH: Fresh cheese is made when the curds have not been pressed or aged. The moisture level in this cheese is high, so fresh cheese tends to have a shorter shelf life. Some common fresh cheeses include feta, mozzarella, and burrata.

SOFT: Soft cheese also has a creamy texture but develops a rind. Some common soft cheeses include brie, camembert, and Humboldt Fog.

SEMISOFT: Semisoft describes cheese that is soft but not gooey. Some examples are gorgonzola, fontina, and havarti.

SEMIHARD: Semihard cheeses are typically aged anywhere between one and six months. The texture is firm yet springy. They are known for their unique taste and aroma. Some common semihard cheeses include cheddar and gruyère.

HARD: Hard cheese is firm, aged from six to thirty-six months (or longer). The longer they age, the stronger the flavors become. They'll also become less creamy and more grainy, losing most of the moisture. Some common hard cheeses are Parmigiano-Reggiano, aged gouda, and Manchego.

COW'S MILK

Cow's milk is responsible for some of the most popular types of cheese. Cows produce milk all year round, and their milk has a high fat content. This cheese typically has a yellow hue and a grassy, earthy, or nutty flavor profile. The style of cheese varies due to the aging process. Some examples of cow's milk cheese include blue cheese, brie, burrata, camembert, cheddar, Comté, gouda, gruyère, parmesan, ricotta, and Taleggio.

GOAT MILK

Goat milk produces a light-colored cheese with a distinct tangy and slightly sweet flavor. Because of its low lactose content, goat cheese is also great for anyone who is lactose intolerant or otherwise struggles with cow's milk. Examples of goat milk cheese include Brabander, bûcheron, chèvre, goat brie, goat feta, goat gouda, soft-ripened goat cheese, and Valençay.

SHEEP'S MILK

Sheep's milk cheese shares a distinct flavor profile, often described as woolly or savory. The flavor can range from light caramel notes to intense roasted meat, depending on how long it ages. Examples of sheep's milk cheese include feta, Halloumi, Manchego, Oussau-Iraty, Pecorino Romano, Pecorino Toscano, Petit Basque, ricotta salata, and Roquefort.

BUFFALO MILK

Water buffalo milk has twice the amount of fat as cow's milk, producing a lush, slightly sweeter cheese. Italy is the leading producer of buffalo milk cheese. Examples of buffalo milk cheese include buffalo milk camembert, burrata, Casatica di Bufala, Mozzarella di Buffalo, and Stracciatella di Bufala.

PLANT-BASED CHEESE

Plant-based cheese can be made from a wide variety of ingredients including tree nuts, soy, coconut, tapioca, and aquafaba (the liquid left over from cooked chickpeas).

Some examples of plant-based cheese include aged artisanal nut cheese, cultured cashew wheels, vegan cream cheese, vegan mozzarella, and vegan parmesan.

the therapeutic art of cutting cheese

There are many different ways to cut cheese. When serving a cheese plate, I usually like to precut harder cheeses while leaving the softer cheeses intact. Here's a guide to the most popular cheese knives.

THE FORK-TIPPED SPEAR goes best with firm cheeses.

THE SMALL SPADE KNIFE is useful for breaking up chunks of very hard cheeses.

THE SOFT CHEESE KNIFE is best for cutting (you guessed it!) soft cheeses like brie.

THE SKELETON KNIFE is perfect for cutting soft, gooey cheeses.

THE FLAT CHEESE KNIFE can be used for shaving and cubing firm cheeses.

THE CHEESE PLANER KNIFE is great for cutting semihard cheeses.

THE GORGONZOLA KNIFE is used to spread soft blue cheeses.

Cutting cheese takes time and precision. To me, cutting cheese is a therapeutic activity. Something about the way it feels to physically dive into the different textures and shapes with a cheese knife is oddly satisfying. Have you ever watched an ASMR (autonomous sensory meridian response) video on the Internet? If not, google it. You'll get what I mean. Let's cut the cheese!

cheese cutting guide

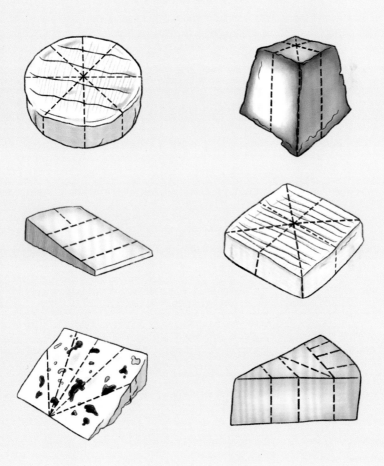

that BACK TO BASICS plate

Using cheese you can find at your local grocery store,
this is the perfect starter plate for a cheese plate beginner.

Key: The Plate: Rectangular wooden board, 11 × 17 inches

1: CHEESE

Manchego

Brie

Cheddar

2: MEAT

*Genoa salami
(sliced, and
sliced in half)*

3: PRODUCE

Dried apricots

Blackberries

Raspberries

Blueberries

4: CRUNCH

Pistachios

Mixed nuts

Flatbread crackers

5: DIP

Fig jam

6: GARNISH

Fresh sage

Fresh rosemary

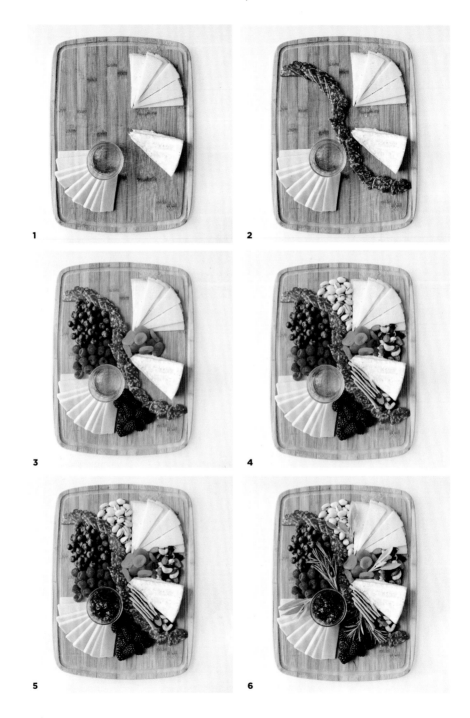

This epic spread will impress any gathering with gourmet cheeses representing three distinct flavors, alongside colorful pairings that pop on the plate.

Key: The Plate: Round wooden lazy Susan, 15-inch diameter

1: CHEESE

Comeback Cow (cow's milk camembert)

Marieke Gouda Mature (semisoft cow's milk cheese)

Cabot Clothbound Cheddar (semihard cow's milk cheese)

2: MEAT

Calabrese (spicy salami)

Prosciutto

3: PRODUCE

Fresh figs

Raspberries

Dried apricots

Blackberries

Blueberries

Castelvetrano olives

4: CRUNCH

Mixed nuts

Butter crackers

5: DIP

Quince jam

6: GARNISH

Fresh thyme

Goat cheese is my favorite, so this cheese plate is truly the Greatest of All Time. With three types of cheese of all different ages paired with springtime produce, this plate takes you on a journey through the world of goat cheese.

....

Key: The Plate: Square slate board, 12 × 12 inches

....

1: CHEESE

Lightly Marinated Goat Cheese with Red Pepper and Herbs (recipe on page 53)

Truffle Tremor (soft-ripened goat cheese with truffles)

Bonne Bouche (bloomy rind goat cheese)

2: MEAT

Prosciutto di Parma

3: PRODUCE

Strawberries

Sugar snap peas

Asparagus

4: CRUNCH

Flatbread crackers

Mixed nuts

5: DIP

Organic honey

6: GARNISH

Yellow mini roses

Fresh thyme

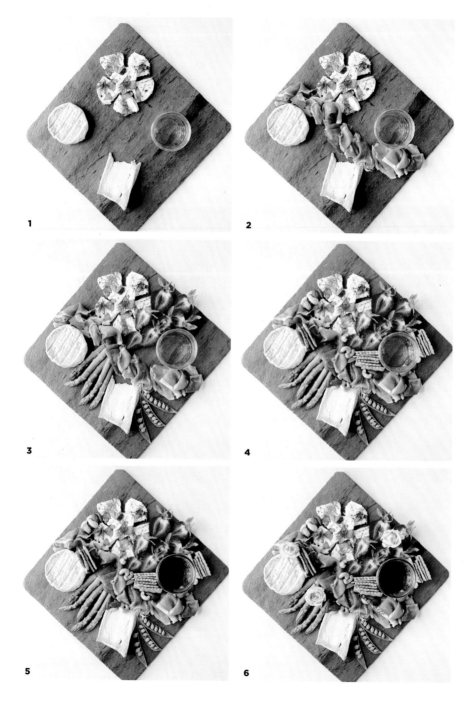

that J'ADORE FROMAGE plate

It's time for an homage to fromage. From a gooey Brie Fermier to a stinky Maroilles, this plate covers a range of French cheeses accompanied by authentic French accoutrements. Bon appétit!

Key: The Plate: Round soapstone with brass handles, 12-inch diameter

1: CHEESE
Maroilles
Comté Saint Antoine
Brie Fermier

2: MEAT
Saucisson
Chicken liver mousse

3: PRODUCE
Cornichons
Red radishes

4: CRUNCH
French baguette
Pistachios

5: DIP
Fresh raspberry jam

6: GARNISH
Fresh thyme
Pink mini roses

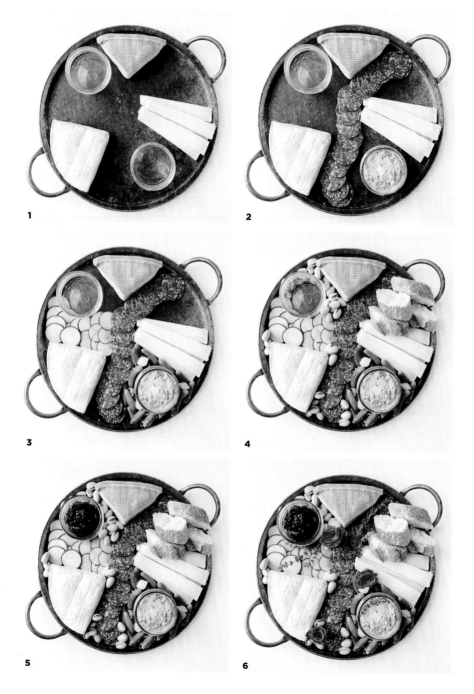

Gather your friends for a perfect summer gathering.
This plate has a range of delicious cheeses and refreshing
fruits to help you enjoy those extra hours of sunshine.

Key: The Plate: Rectangular wooden cutting board, 10 × 14 inches

1: CHEESE

*Midnight Moon
(goat gouda)*

*Tapping Reeve
(colonial-style cow's
milk cheese)*

*Coperthwaite
(camembert)*

Irish cheddar

2: MEAT

Genoa salami, sliced

3: PRODUCE

Blood oranges

Blackberries

Blueberries

Raspberries

4: CRUNCH

*Pepita, almond,
walnut, and cranberry
mix*

Herb crackers

5: DIP

*Black cherry
preserves*

6: GARNISH

Pink mini roses

Fresh rosemary

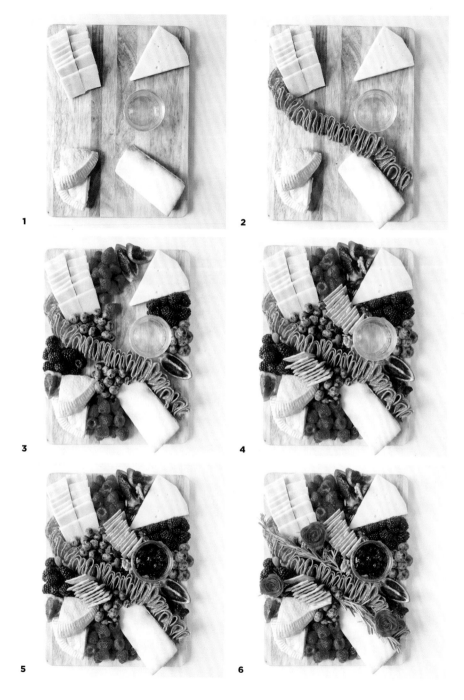

Transport yourself to the Italian countryside with this decadent buffalo mozzarella plate. You can substitute buratta or cow's milk mozzarella as well!

1: CHEESE

Buffalo Mozzarella with Roasted Tomatoes and Balsamic Glaze (recipe on page 54)

2: MEAT

Prosciutto

3: PRODUCE

Tomatoes on the vine

Fresh figs

Grape tomatoes (red and orange)

4: CRUNCH

Toasted French baguette with olive oil and herbs

5: DIP

Pesto

6: GARNISH

Fresh basil

Life is all about balance. The yin and yang. In this case,
our yin is cultured cashew cheese and our yang is a Salami River.
Best of both worlds for our dairy-free friends!

Key: The Plate: Round plastic platter, 12-inch diameter

1: CHEESE

*Truffle Cultured
Cashew wheel*

*Carrot Cultured
Cashew wheel*

2: MEAT

Barolo salami

3: PRODUCE

Dragon fruit

Blackberries

Blueberries

Raspberries

Asparagus

Persian cucumbers

Red radishes

4: CRUNCH

Flatbread crackers

Pistachios

5: DIP

N/A

6: GARNISH

Fresh thyme

Blue thistle flowers

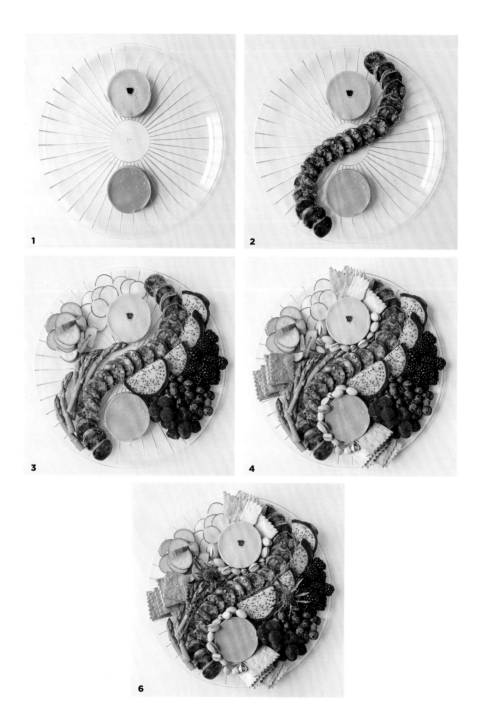

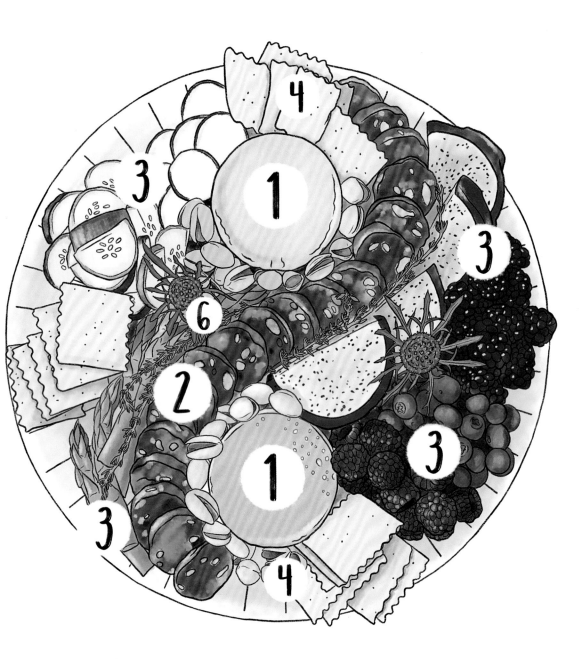

that
BRIE
MINE
plate ♡ ♡

The perfect plate for entertaining. Place this ovenproof
dish directly in the oven to bake the brie, let it cool some, and then pair
it with all of your favorite wintry sides, especially some crispy bread
to dip into the gooey brie.

Key: The Plate: Rectangular ceramic or glass baking dish, 8 × 12 inches

1: CHEESE

*Baked Brie with
Caramelized Pears,
Toasted Walnuts, and
Pomegranate Seeds
(recipe on page 57)*

2: MEAT

Genoa salami, sliced

3: PRODUCE

*Pomegranates
Anjou pears
Gala apples*

4: CRUNCH

*Pepitas
Mixed nuts
French baguette
Flatbread crackers*

5: DIP

N/A

6: GARNISH

*Fresh rosemary
Fresh thyme*

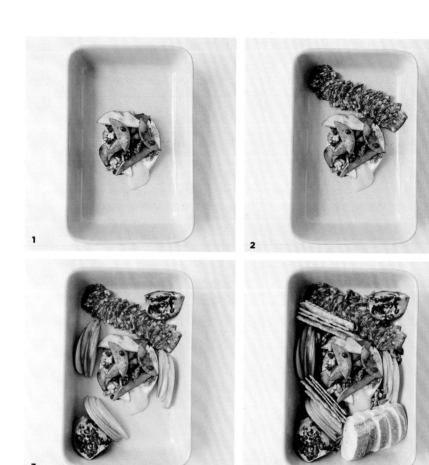

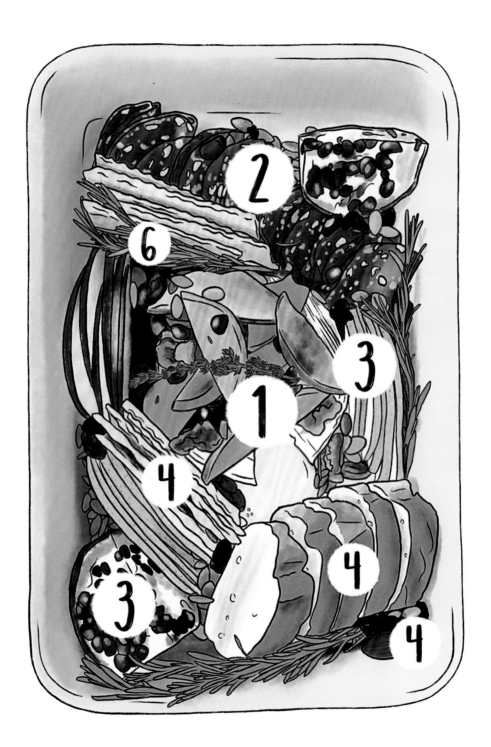

lightly marinated goat cheese
with red pepper and herbs

(featured on That G.O.A.T. Plate, page 28)

I love fresh goat cheese. It's the perfect cheese to spice up as it easily absorbs other flavors that complement its natural tanginess. Here I put my own spin on marinated goat cheese, and it's incredibly easy to make. This cheese is lightly marinated (so the oil doesn't make a mess on the cheese plate) with fresh herbs and a punch of lemon and chile.

Serves 8 to 10

1 (8-ounce) log plain goat cheese

1½ tablespoons chopped fresh dill

1½ tablespoons chopped fresh basil

½ teaspoon crushed red pepper flakes

1½ teaspoons fresh lemon juice

1 cup extra-virgin olive oil

Coarse salt and freshly ground black pepper to taste

1. Cut the goat cheese into ⅓-inch-thick slices and place them in a 9 × 13-inch baking dish or glass container with a lid. (I like to pop my goat cheese log in the freezer for about 15 minutes before slicing to ensure clean cuts.)

2. In a large measuring cup, mix the dill, basil, red pepper flakes, lemon juice, and olive oil until blended.

3. Pour just enough of the olive oil mixture over the goat cheese so there is a light layer covering the bottom of the dish. You don't want to completely submerge the cheese in oil.

4. Cover and let the cheese marinate in the fridge for up to 3 hours.

5. Remove the slices from the oil and sprinkle with coarse salt and freshly ground pepper. Serve them on your cheese plate with crackers or bread for dipping.

buffalo mozzarella with roasted tomatoes and balsamic glaze

(featured on That Fresh Mozz Plate, page 40)

Nothing compares to the lush and slightly sweet flavor of buffalo mozzarella. I tried my first real buffalo mozzarella on a cool summer night at a small side-street café in Italy. (You know when you try a cheese that's so good, you can still taste it from memory? Now I can't stop tasting mozzarella as I write this.) Tomatoes, herbs, and balsamic glaze are classic pairings with mozzarella, and they add an extra Italian flair. If you can't find buffalo mozzarella at the store, cow's milk mozzarella will do the trick.

Serves 4 to 6

2 garlic cloves, sliced

3 sprigs fresh thyme

1 cup cherry or grape tomatoes, halved

1 teaspoon olive oil

Coarse salt and freshly ground black pepper to taste

1 (8-ounce) ball buffalo mozzarella

1½ tablespoons chopped fresh basil

Balsamic glaze, for drizzling

1. Preheat the oven to 300°F. Arrange the garlic, thyme, and halved tomatoes, cut sides up, on a foil-lined baking sheet. Drizzle with a light coating of olive oil and season with salt and pepper. Roast for 25 minutes, until the tomatoes are slightly shriveled and browned.

2. Slice the mozzarella in half and set it aside on the cheese plate.

3. Once the tomatoes are roasted, spoon them on top to cover the mozzarella. Sprinkle the basil over the tomatoes and drizzle with the balsamic glaze. Finish with salt and pepper.

baked brie with caramelized pears, toasted walnuts, and pomegranate seeds

(featured on That Brie Mine Plate, page 48)

I'm convinced that baked brie tastes best when the weather is cold and gray. Pears and pomegranates are the perfect winter fruits to provide some extra sweetness in contrast to the savory cheese.

Serves 6 to 8

¼ cup walnuts

1 (8-ounce) wheel brie

2 tablespoons (¼ stick) un-salted butter

¼ cup packed light brown sugar

1 Anjou pear, cored and sliced

¼ teaspoon ground cinnamon

1 tablespoon pomegranate seeds

1. Preheat the oven to 350°F. Place an oven rack in the center of the oven. Place another rack above it.

2. Scatter the walnuts on a baking sheet and place it on the upper rack. Toast for 5 to 7 minutes and remove from the oven; let cool, then roughly chop.

3. Unwrap the brie and place it directly in an 8 × 12-inch baking dish.

4. Bake on the middle rack for 12 to 14 minutes, until soft to the touch.

5. Meanwhile, heat a medium-size skillet over medium heat and melt the butter. When it begins to bubble, stir in the sugar and cook just until it dissolves, about 3 minutes.

6. Add the pear slices and cook, stirring gently. Cook until the pear is lightly browned, about 3 minutes. Fold in the cinnamon and remove the skillet from the heat.

7. Remove the brie from the oven and let cool for 5 minutes. Top with pears, walnuts. Sprinkle the pomegranate seeds on top. Serve at once with crusty bread.

2

THE SALAMI RIVER AND BEYOND

The food we eat can delight us each day. There's nothing like a memorable eating experience—one that causes you to stop and savor the moment. Our appreciation for cured meats grew out of the three and a half years we lived in Parma, Italy, prosciutto's area of origin. We saw how the careful treatment of fine materials resulted in an accessible, sublime, and entirely regional cuisine. Great food satisfies the senses and the body, the emotions and the mind.

—HERB AND KATHY ECKHOUSE, CO-FOUNDERS OF LA QUERCIA

Now for step 2 of the Cheese By Numbers method. Once the cheese is on the plate, it's time to add the meat. Meat can come in all shapes and sizes, and doesn't necessarily have to come from an animal (shout-out, fig salami). Cured meats are a popular addition to a cheese board, adding another layer of texture and robust flavor. I'm a total meat lover and use a wide range of cured and smoked meats like prosciutto, salami, bresaola, saucisson, and chorizo, or, if I'm feeling more creative, smoked salmon, deviled eggs, chicken wings, and shrimp. Pairing meat with cheese can be simple, as they're both full of fat, protein, and salt. Think about balancing shared flavors with contrasting elements. For example, Pecorino Toscano and prosciutto: They're both salty, but the textures are completely different. Opposite flavors can also attract: with the chicken wings on That Game Day Plate (page 92), the acidic bite of hot sauce is cut with the pungent creaminess of blue cheese.

the salami river

The Salami River is a key stylistic choice to set your plate apart. Embrace the art of folding meat and mindfully placing it on the cheese plate in a way that creates movement and flow, like a river. Let the Salami River be a tranquil and meditative activity, a time to embrace pattern and symmetry. The process is simple: Start with presliced salami. Fold each slice in half, and in half again, creating a triangular shape (salami origami!). Press a few folded slices in your hand so they hold together. Lay the salami down on the plate, then repeat until the Salami River spans from one end to the other, gracefully flowing through the board. If you're working with a piece of hard salami, cut the log into ⅓-inch slices and layer them on the plate in a similar flowing shape. You can create rivers out of any cured meat, or even a "cucumber river" out of sliced cucumbers for a vegetarian option.

PRO TIP: For prosciutto, remove each slice of meat from the package and gently lay them on the plate, rippling and folding the slices to create a wavy texture. If you're working with bulkier meat like steak or chicken, you can create a "meat mountain" instead of a river, filling in one section of the plate.

The Salami River also plays the important role of mapping out the various elements on the plate. Use it to separate fruits and vegetables, with sweet berries on one side and briny olives and cornichons on the other. Or use it to divide the colors on the board, creating contrast between the blues and purples and the greens and yellows. The Salami River is more than just meat on the plate; it's a way to provide balance amid the chaos.

your go-to meat guide

The key here is to choose items you enjoy, and don't be afraid to get creative! Meat and cheese are like a married couple, so you can't really go wrong pairing the two.

PORK

The humble pig provides us with some of the most popular meats on a cheese plate. Often aged or cured in the Italian or French style, pork provides a wide range of textures and flavors for your cheese plate creation. Some examples of pork include chorizo, *jamon iberico,* mortadella, pepperoni, prosciutto, salami (genoa, herbed, or peppered salami), saucisson, and soppressata.

BEEF

Beef is a bit less common on a cheese plate, but there are some delicious cooked and aged beef products out there. If the spirit moves you, grill up a steak for your cheese plate! It'll go great with blue cheese. Some examples of beef include beef salami, bresaola, pastrami, roast beef, and steak.

POULTRY

Feel free to experiment with poultry pairings, like fried chicken or deviled eggs. Some other examples of poultry include chicken liver mousse, chicken sausage, and hard-boiled eggs.

FISH

Smoked fish is a great addition to a breakfast board. Like charcuterie, smoked fish is salty and fatty, and it adds an interesting flavor profile and texture. Some examples of fish include grilled shrimp or shrimp cocktail, smoked salmon, and smoked whitefish.

PLANT-BASED

I always love having a plant-based option for balance. Some examples of vegan "meat" include fig salami, vegan deli slices, vegan sausage, and vegan bacon.

that
SALAMI
RIVER
plate

Put your Salami River skills to the test. With three types of meat, the textures and colors flow gracefully down through the center of the plate.

Key: The Plate: Round wooden tray, 15-inch diameter

1: CHEESE

Blue

Asiago d'Allevo (Italian hard cow's milk cheese)

Jarlsberg (Norwegian semisoft cow's milk cheese)

2: MEAT

Genoa salami, sliced

Finocchiona (fennel salami)

Borsellino salami (chile-spiced salami)

3: PRODUCE

Green olives

Cornichons

Peppadew peppers

Dried apricots

4: CRUNCH

Wheat crackers

Walnuts

Almonds

Pistachios

5: DIP

Whole-grain mustard

6: GARNISH

Fresh rosemary

Fresh thyme

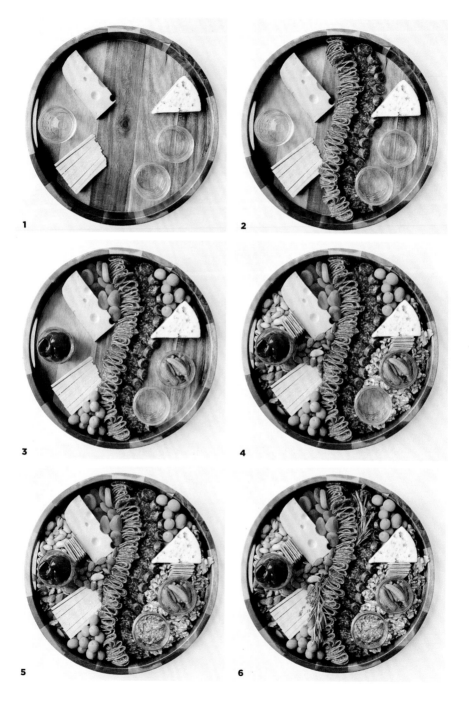

that ITALIAN COUNTRYSIDE plate

Go on a tour through the most delicious Italian cured meats, with fresh sliced prosciutto and savory mortadella.

Key: The Plate: Round porcelain plate, 11-inch diameter

1: CHEESE

Parmigiano-Reggiano

Mini mozzarella balls

2: MEAT

Speck

Mortadella

*Prosciutto di
San Daniele*

3: PRODUCE

Champagne grapes

Castelvetrano olives

4: CRUNCH

Breadsticks

Marcona almonds

Taralli *crackers
(Italian oval crackers)*

5: DIP

Balsamic glaze

6: GARNISH

Fresh oregano

Fresh basil

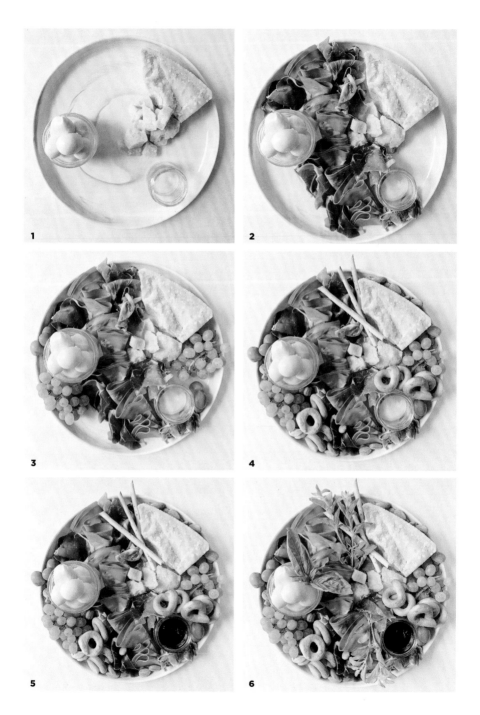

70 / THAT CHEESE PLATE WILL CHANGE YOUR LIFE

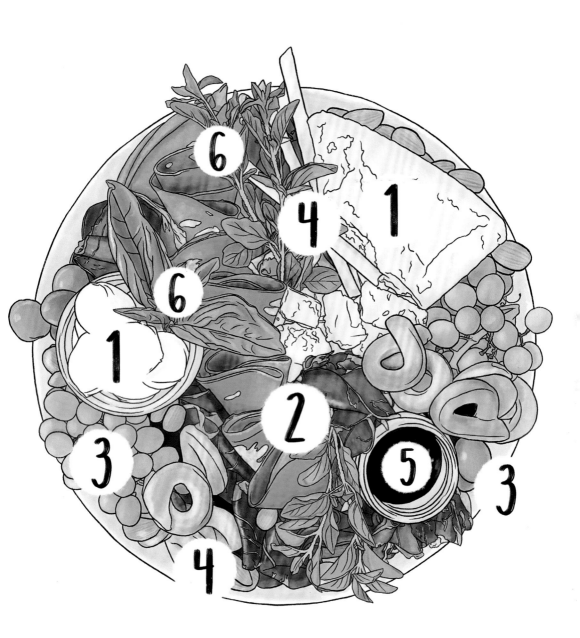

that FIGLAMI RIVER plate

For my vegetarian friends, I created a "figlami" river.
You can also use vegan deli meats or supplement with produce
(cucumber river, anyone?).

Key: The Plate: Square slate board, 12 × 12 inches

1: CHEESE

Havarti

Gruyère

2: MEAT

Vegan fig salami (pistachio cinnamon)

3: PRODUCE

Peaches

Fresh apricots

Rainier cherries

4: CRUNCH

Flatbread crackers

Walnuts

5: DIP

Organic honey

6: GARNISH

Yellow pansies

Fresh thyme

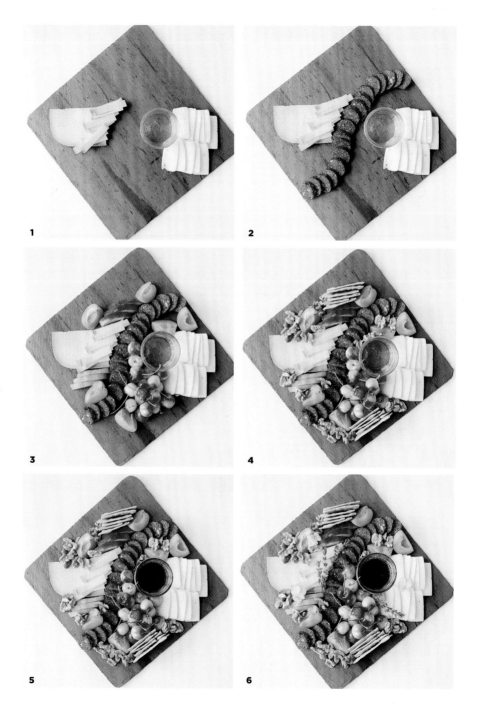

that SUMMER IN THE CITY plate

Stop by your local farmers' market and pick up these
items for a bountiful plate for entertaining.

Key: The Plate: Rectangular wooden board, 11 × 17 inches

1: CHEESE

*Mini mozzarella
balls*

Sharp cheddar

2: MEAT

Genoa salami, sliced

*Prosciutto-Wrapped
Melon with Goat
Cheese and Basil
(recipe on page 97)*

3: PRODUCE

Green grapes

Dried apricots

Raspberries

Peaches

4: CRUNCH

Walnuts

Water crackers

5: DIP

*Strawberry rhubarb
jam*

6: GARNISH

Nasturtiums

Fresh basil

Marigolds

Pansies

Fresh thyme

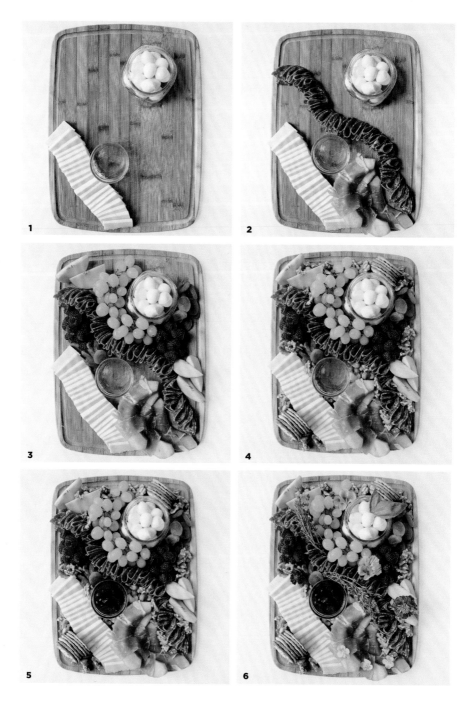

that GRILL NIGHT *plate*

Grilled marinated shrimp finds its way onto a
cheese plate for a delicious dinner cheese board.

Key: The Plate: Round wooden lazy Susan, 15-inch diameter

1: CHEESE

Feta

Grilled Halloumi

2: MEAT

*Grilled Marinated
Shrimp Skewers
with Feta (recipe
on page 98)*

3: PRODUCE

*Grape tomatoes
(red and yellow)*

Limes

Persian cucumbers

Watermelon

Fresh jalapeños

Red radishes

4: CRUNCH

Marcona almonds

Breadsticks

French baguette

5: DIP

*Marinade (set aside
from shrimp recipe)*

6: GARNISH

Fresh cilantro

Zinnias

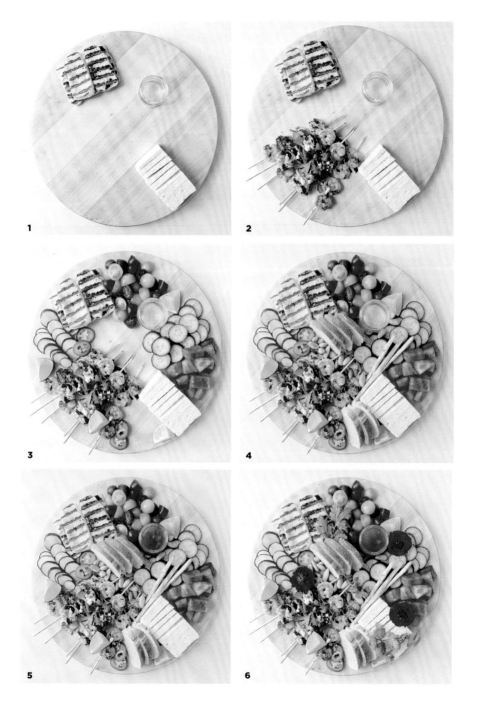

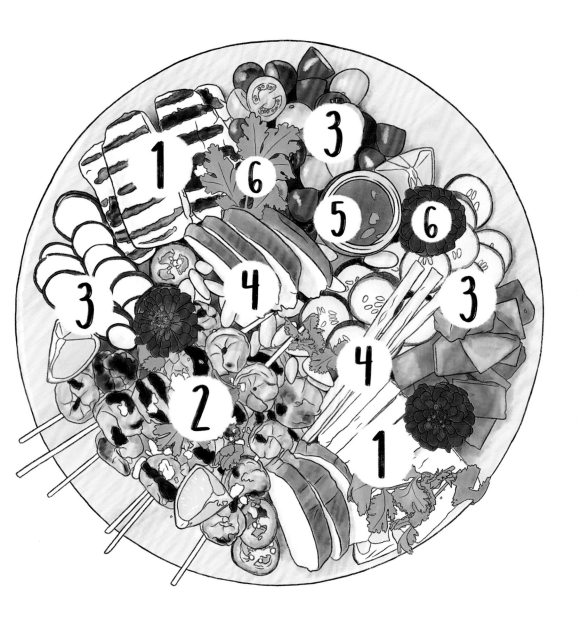

that
PICNIC-TO-GO
plate

Bring the Salami River to an actual river with this
personal plate you can pack up and take anywhere.

Key: The Plate: Rectangular glass baking dish, 5 × 8 inches

1: CHEESE
Comté

2: MEAT
Genoa salami, sliced

3: PRODUCE
Strawberries
Dried apricots
Castelvetrano olives

4: CRUNCH
Marcona almonds
Seeded crackers
Walnuts

5: DIP
Blueberry jam

6: GARNISH
Fresh thyme
Carnations

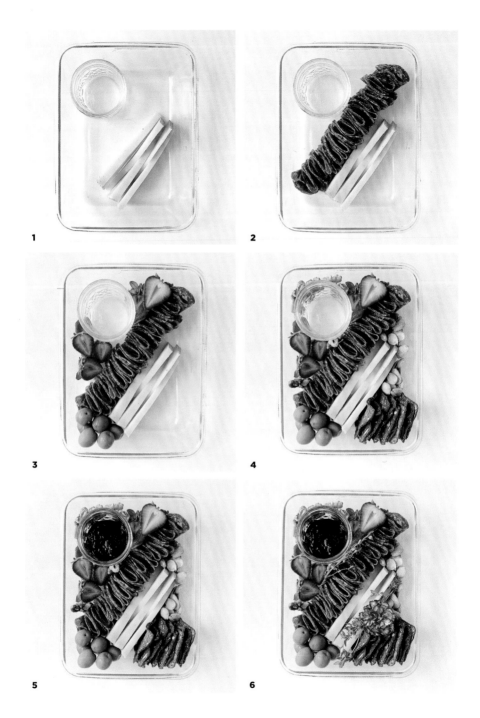

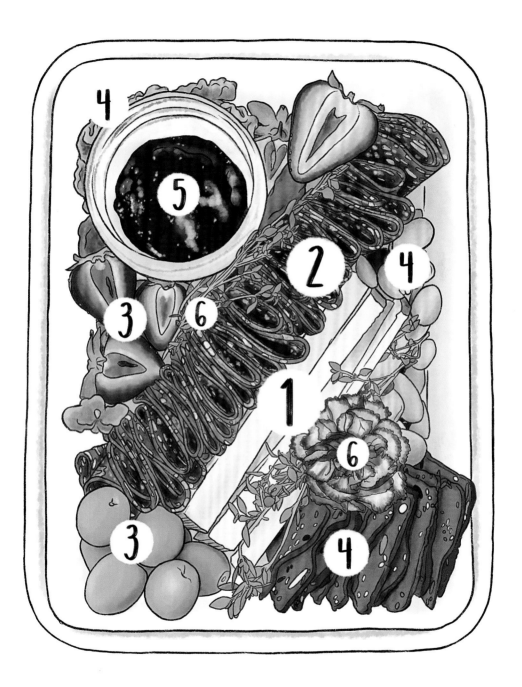

Make new friends with a plate of charcuterie.

Key: The Plate: Round slate board, 12-inch diameter

1: CHEESE

*Keep Dreaming
(cow's milk
camembert)*

*Midnight Moon
(goat gouda)*

2: MEAT

Hard salami, sliced

Prosciutto di Parma

Soppressata, sliced

3: PRODUCE

Dried apricots

Blueberries

Blackberries

4: CRUNCH

Almonds

Cashews

5: DIP

Fig jam

6: GARNISH

Fresh rosemary

Yellow carnations

Fresh thyme

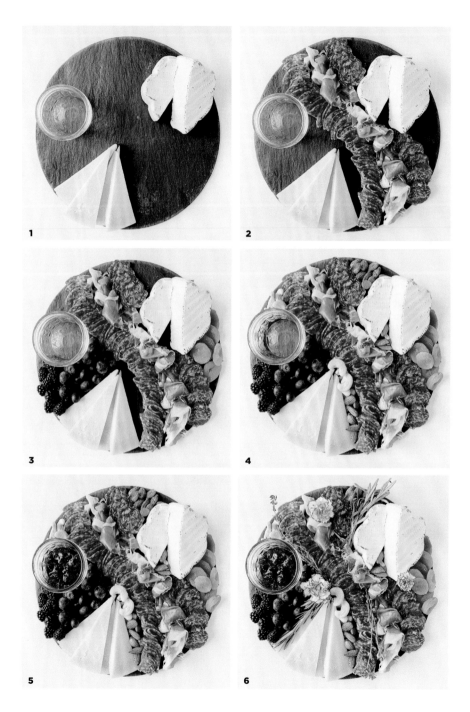

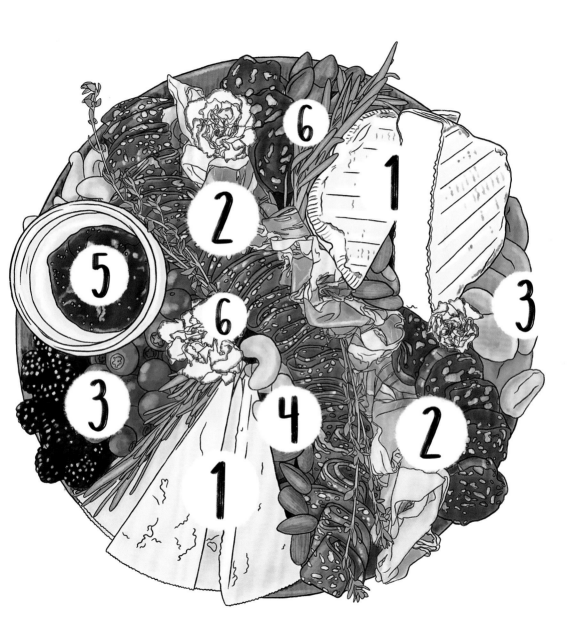

that
GAME
DAY
plate

It's time to whip out the wings. Game day
calls for an epic cheese plate.

Key: The Plate: Rectangular plastic tray, 10 × 15 inches

1: CHEESE

Pepper Jack

Taleggio

2: MEAT

Chorizo

Fried chicken wings

3: PRODUCE

Celery

Fresh jalapeños

*Mini sweet peppers
(orange, red,
and yellow)*

*Rainbow baby
carrots*

4: CRUNCH

Spicy almonds

Potato chips

5: DIP

Buffalo sauce

Blue cheese dressing

6: GARNISH

Fresh rosemary

Fresh chives

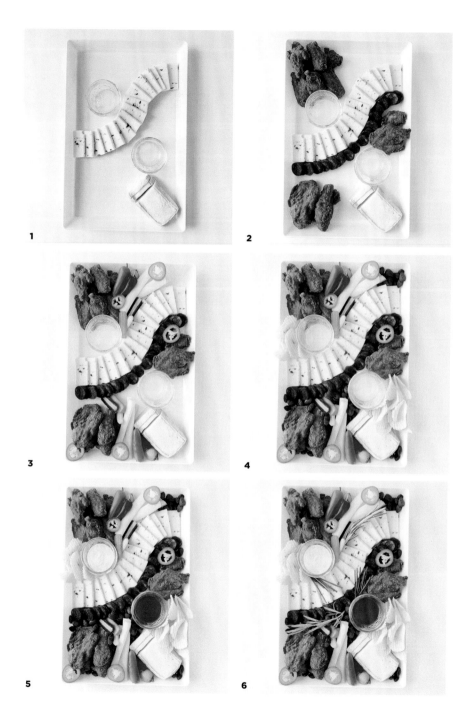

prosciutto-wrapped melon with goat cheese and basil

(featured on That Summer in the City Plate, page 76)

This is a delicious, colorful, classic summer snack that pairs beautifully with crumbled goat cheese. The sweet melon perfectly complements the salty prosciutto. And, as an added bonus, it's probably one of the easiest recipes in this book, made of simple items you can find at your local grocery store, dressed up to impress your guests.

Serves 6 to 8

1 ripe cantaloupe

1 (4-ounce) package sliced prosciutto

¼ cup crumbled goat cheese

2 tablespoons thinly sliced fresh basil leaves, for garnish

½ teaspoon freshly ground black pepper

1. With a sharp knife, cut the cantaloupe in half lengthwise. Scoop out and discard the seeds. Slice one of the halves lengthwise into slender wedges and cut off the rind.

2. Tear the prosciutto lengthwise into 2-inch-wide strips and wrap them around each melon slice. Arrange the wrapped melon slices on your cheese plate.

3. With a spoon, sprinkle a light layer of crumbled goat cheese over the melon. Garnish with the sliced basil and sprinkle with the pepper.

4. Serve and enjoy! If you're prepping this ahead of time, cover the plate and refrigerate until ready to serve.

grilled marinated shrimp skewers with feta

(featured on That Grill Night Plate, page 80)

I have a theory that most food tastes better on a skewer. This specifically applies to shrimp, seasoned and blackened on the grill. This summer staple was inspired by my dad, whose self-care is grilling.

Serves 8 to 10

10 8-inch bamboo skewers

½ cup extra-virgin olive oil

1 teaspoon honey

Juice of 2 limes

2 tablespoons chopped fresh cilantro, plus more for garnish

2 garlic cloves, minced

¼ teaspoon kosher salt

¼ teaspoon freshly ground black pepper

1 pound large fresh shrimp, peeled and deveined

¼ cup crumbled feta cheese

1. If using a grill (not a grill pan), soak bamboo skewers in water for 45 minutes, or use metal skewers.

2. In a small bowl, whisk together the olive oil, honey, lime juice, cilantro, garlic, salt, and pepper. Set ¼ cup of the marinade aside.

3. Place the shrimp in a ziplock bag or glass baking dish. Cover completely with the marinade, toss, and seal. Marinate in the refrigerator for 30 minutes.

4. Set the grill or grill pan to medium-high heat.

5. Remove the shrimp from the refrigerator and discard the marinade. Thread 4 shrimp onto each skewer.

6. Grill for 3 to 4 minutes on each side, until the shrimp just turn pink and opaque.

7. Place the skewers on the plate. Top with the crumbled feta and garnish with chopped cilantro. Serve the cheese plate with the reserved marinade in a ramekin.

3

PAINTING
WITH
PRODUCE

What inspires me most are the seasons. I love cooking seasonally and with fresh produce. Fruit in the summer; veggies, decadent desserts and cozy dinners in the fall; warmers and hearty soups in winter; and fresh spring eats. I love that with every new season I get to make new and exciting things with fresh ingredients.

—TIEGHAN GERARD,
CREATOR OF HALF BAKED HARVEST

Once the Salami River is flowing, it's time for step 3, produce! Mix and match flavors, textures, and colors. Fruit can be a sweet contrast to salty cheese, while vegetables act as an earthy, neutral ground, bringing flavor without overpowering the palate. The fruits and veggies also provide the ultimate balance to the fat and salt. When you eat well, you feel well. Fruits and vegetables cover the spectrum of the rainbow and beyond, so take the opportunity to engage your senses with color and get creative. Find the colors that inspire you and paint that cheese plate like the masterpiece it is.

shop local

I love shopping local at the farmers' market. It's the perfect way to get outside and support your community. Knowing where the produce is grown, meeting the farmers, and learning about seasonal produce is not just educational, it's good for the soul. Farmers' markets are also important in rebuilding local food economies, providing a cost-effective opportunity for farms to make a profit and encounter new communities of buyers. It's an opportunity to come together and learn about locally grown produce.

dried fruits and pickled veggies

I'm a big fan of dried fruits and pickled vegetables on a cheese plate, especially in the winter months. Some of my favorite dried fruits include apricots, figs, and cranberries, which all add a sweet and tart contrast to salty, buttery cheese and a rustic visual element to the plate. Jarred pickled veggies, like cornichons and olives, are great all year round as well, providing a slight crunch and some tang from the brine. You can also make your own pickled vegetables (a new favorite hobby of mine ever since I discovered how easy it is). You'll find a recipe for quick pickles on page 140.

thoughtful prep and placement

Cutting produce is key to ensuring your guests can graze with ease. Prep may take a while, but this step is an opportunity to practice mindfulness. Focus your energy on the task at hand: Observe the colors and details of the produce. Taste the sweetness of the fresh raspberries, the bitter crunch of the radishes, the citrus bite of the grapefruit. Bring your senses back to the practice. Once all of your produce is prepped, it's ready for the plate. You can arrange produce in a variety of ways. Like your Salami River, build "produce ponds" to offset different parts of your cheese board: scatter small piles of like produce across the board.

that FRESH-PICKED plate

This is an approachable, fresh plate with produce from the grocery store. The plate is easy to build with just one type of cheese and an array of color.

Key: The Plate: Rectangular porcelain plate, 6 × 10 inches

1: CHEESE

Coupole (soft-ripened goat cheese)

2: MEAT

N/A

3: PRODUCE

Grape tomatoes (red and orange)

Red radishes

English cucumbers

Fresh figs

Raspberries

Blackberries

Blueberries

4: CRUNCH

Mixed nuts

5: DIP

Fresh raspberry jam

6: GARNISH

Fresh thyme

Dried thistle flowers

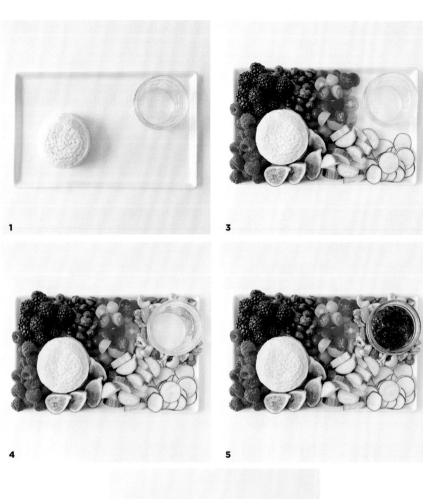

that PLANT PARTY plate

It's a plant-based celebration! Spread the joy
of a cheese plate packed with nutrients,
good for the body and mind.

Key: The Plate: Rectangular wooden board, 11 × 17 inches

1: CHEESE

*Rosemary Cultured
Cashew wheel*

*Truffle Cultured
Cashew wheel*

*"Everything" flavored
cashew cream cheese*

2: MEAT

N/A

3: PRODUCE

*Grape tomatoes
(red, orange,
and yellow)*

White nectarines

Persian cucumbers

Purple cauliflower

Yellow cauliflower

Blackberries

Blueberries

4: CRUNCH

Mixed nuts

Gluten-free crackers

5: DIP

Mixed-berry jam

6: GARNISH

Fresh rosemary

Dried lavender

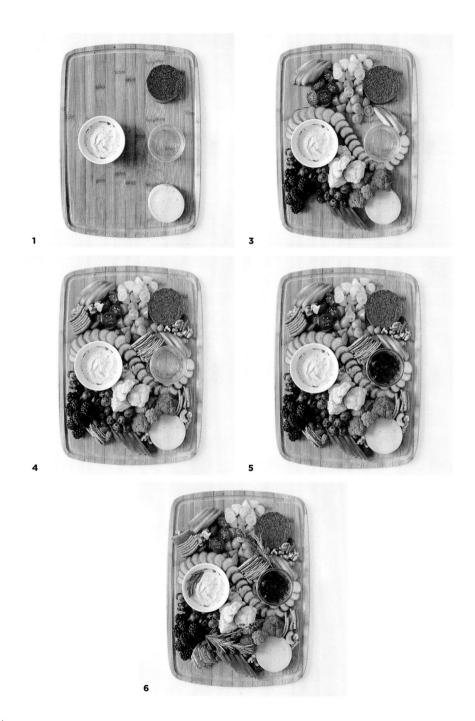

Fill your plate with fresh produce (and cheese!)
from the farm. A journey to the farmers'
market is always worth it.

Key: The Plate: Round wooden board with handle, 10-inch diameter

---

1: CHEESE

Alpine-style cow's milk cheese

2: MEAT

Wild boar salami

3: PRODUCE

Purple radishes

Persian cucumbers

Purple carrots

Long radishes

Watermelon radishes

4: CRUNCH

Pistachios

Gluten-free crackers

5: DIP

Local honey

6: GARNISH

Flowering Broccolini

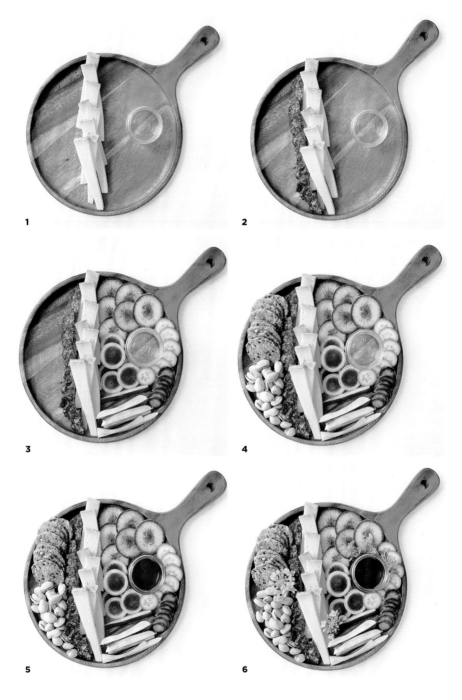

1

2

3

4

5

6

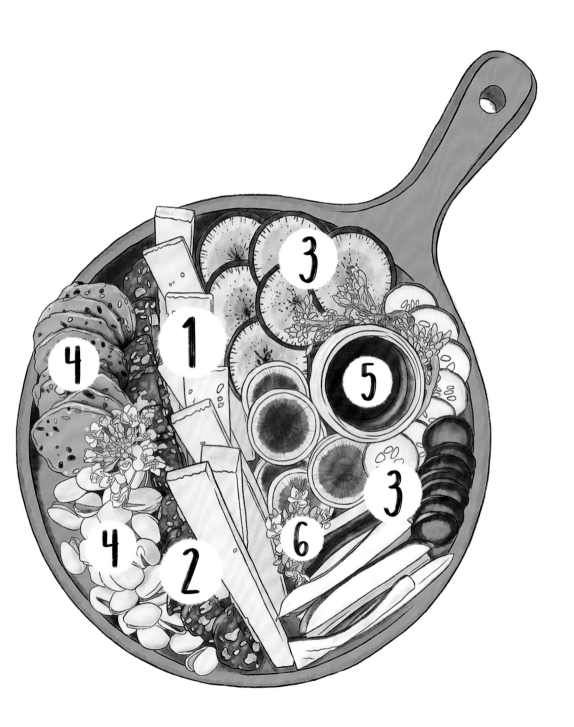

that BEACH PICNIC plate

This is the ideal plate for your sunset
barbecue at the beach. Caprese goes from salad
to skewer with a grilled veggie plate.

Key: The Plate: Round porcelain plate, 11-inch diameter

1: CHEESE

Marinated goat cheese

*Caprese Skewers
with Balsamic Glaze
(recipe on page 139)*

2: MEAT

*Sautéed chicken
sausage*

3: PRODUCE

Persian cucumbers

*Grilled portobello
mushrooms*

Grilled yellow squash

Grilled zucchini

4: CRUNCH

Sourdough bread

5: DIP

Balsamic glaze

6: GARNISH

Flowering Broccolini

Fresh thyme

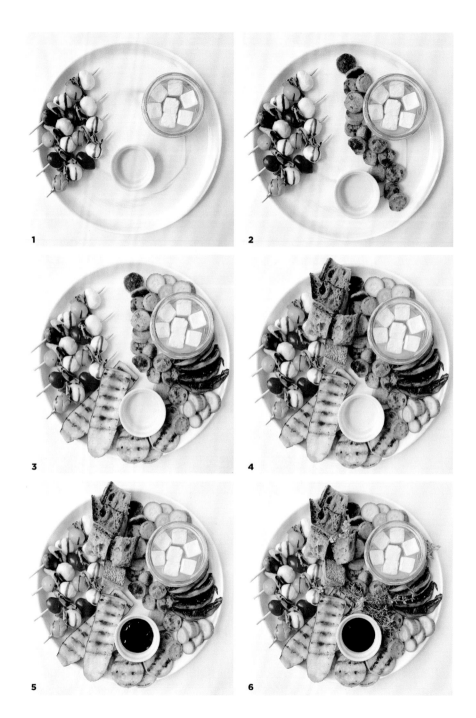

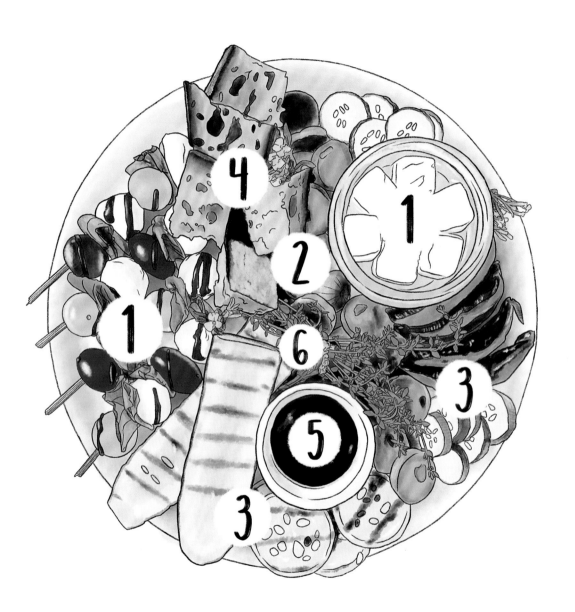

that AUTUMN SPICE plate

This plate has an array of spiced and
dried fruits, the perfect companion for those
crisp autumn months.

Key: The Plate: Round wooden board, 15-inch diameter

1: CHEESE

*Pleasant Ridge
Reserve (aged
alpine-style cow's
milk cheese)*

*Up in Smoke (smoky
goat cheese wrapped
in maple leaves)*

*Harbison (soft cow's
milk cheese)*

2: MEAT

Genoa salami, sliced

3: PRODUCE

Dried apricots

Dried oranges

Fig almond cake

Dried figs

4: CRUNCH

Trail mix

*Cranberry and
pistachio crackers*

Seeded crackers

Walnuts

5: DIP

Fig jam

6: GARNISH

Fresh rosemary

1

2

3

4

5

6

that FIRESIDE plate

Cozy up next to the fireplace and celebrate
the holidays with cheese, gooey cookies,
and winter aromas.

Key: The Plate: Rectangular wooden board, 9½ × 13½ inches

1: CHEESE

Midnight Moon
(goat gouda)

Aged cheddar

Havarti

2: MEAT

Genoa salami, sliced

3: PRODUCE

Raspberries

Red apples

Green grapes

Fresh cranberries

4: CRUNCH

Holiday cookies
(Switch out the cookies
to represent the holiday
of your choice!)

Taralli *crackers
(Italian oval crackers)*

Mixed nuts

5: DIP

Red currant jam

6: GARNISH

Fresh rosemary

Additional fresh
cranberries

Cinnamon sticks

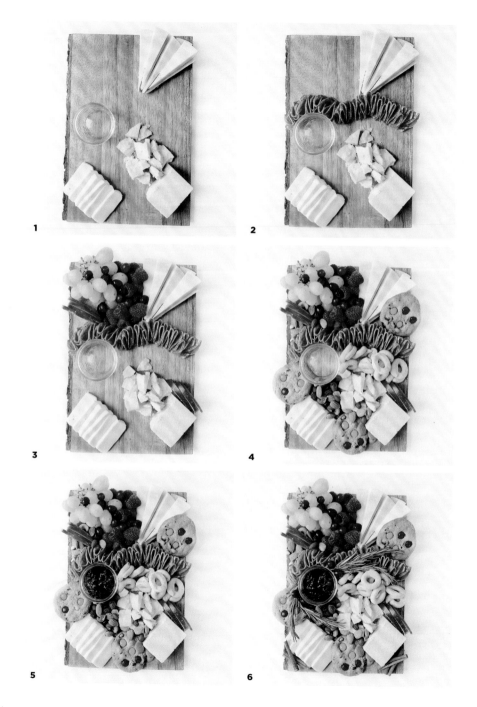

that
SEASON OF LOVE
plate

Proposal? Anniversary? Just a chill night in?
Show your love with this romantic plate.

Key: The Plate: Round slate board, 12-inch diameter

1: CHEESE

*French brie (cut
into a heart shape
with a 3½-inch
cookie cutter)*

2: MEAT

Soppressata, sliced

3: PRODUCE

*Dark Chocolate–
Covered Strawberries
(recipe on page 143)*

Blackberries

Concord grapes

Raspberries

4: CRUNCH

Walnuts

Waffle cookies

5: DIP

Cherry compote

6: GARNISH

Dried rose petals

that
QUICK
PICKLE
plate

Elevate your vegetables with some homemade
quick pickles, which provide the perfect amount of crunch
and acidity to pair with soft cheeses.

Key: The Plate: Square slate board, 12 × 12 inches

1: CHEESE

*St. Agur (French
blue cheese)*

*Comeback Cow (cow's
milk camembert)*

2: MEAT

Prosciutto di Parma

3: PRODUCE

Blueberries

Dried apricots

Persian cucumbers

Red radishes

*That Quick Pickle
(recipe on page 140)*

4: CRUNCH

Wheat crackers

Fruit and nut mix

5: DIP

*Whole-grain
mustard*

6: GARNISH

Fresh dill

Yellow mini roses

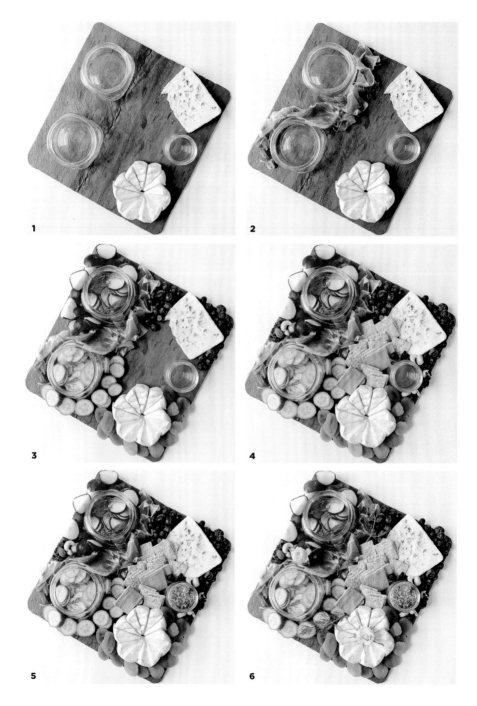

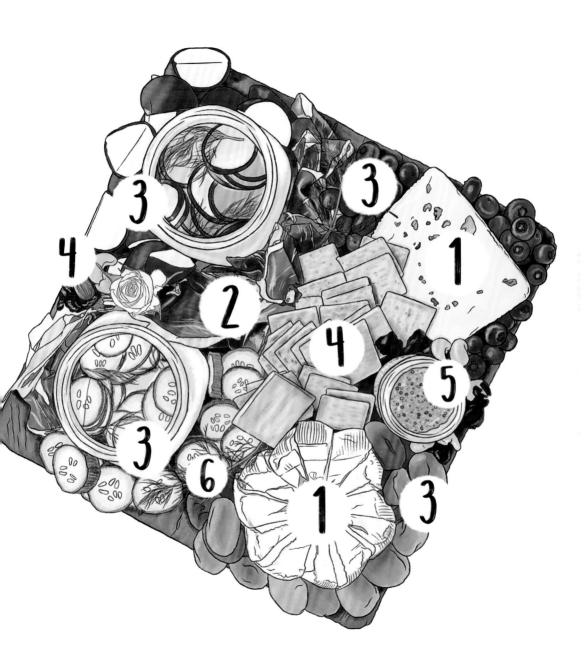

caprese skewers with balsamic glaze

(featured on That Beach Picnic Plate, page 118)

I love fresh mozzarella and tomato on a warm summer evening. This magical combination, paired with basil and a sweet balsamic glaze, is easy and delicious. Take that flavor and put it on a skewer for a fun, bite-size experience!

Makes 6 skewers

6 (4-inch) bamboo skewers

1 pint orange and red grape or cherry tomatoes

Fresh basil leaves

8 ounces mini mozzarella balls, drained and patted dry

¼ cup balsamic glaze

1. Using a skewer, spear the top of one grape tomato and slide it down to about 1 inch from the bottom of the skewer.

2. Fold a small basil leaf in half and slide it next to the tomato.

3. Skewer a mozzarella ball and slide it next to the basil leaf. Repeat with another tomato and folded basil leaf, and end with a mozzarella ball.

4. Repeat steps 1–3 with the remaining ingredients and skewers.

5. Drizzle with the balsamic glaze and serve.

that quick pickle

(featured on That Quick Pickle Plate, page 134)

Put a twist on leftover cheese plate veggies with a simple quick pickle. I used cucumbers and radishes here, but feel free to adapt it for any fresh vegetables, and get creative by adding different herbs and spices! Unlike the texture of canned fermented pickles, quick pickles have a light and refreshing crunch that pairs well with any cheese.

Serves 10

4 Persian cucumbers

2 jars (I used 8-ounce widemouthed mason jars for That Quick Pickle Plate)

8 medium red radishes

1 cup white wine vinegar

½ teaspoon mustard seeds

2 tablespoons kosher salt

1 teaspoon sugar

6 sprigs fresh dill

1. Wash the cucumbers and radishes and slice each ⅛ inch thick, keeping them separate. Place each vegetable in a jar, leaving at least 1 inch of head-space.

2. In a small pot, combine the vinegar and 2 cups water and bring to a simmer over medium heat. Add the mustard seeds, then the salt and sugar and stir until completely dissolved.

3. Pour the hot liquid mixture into the jars, covering the vegetables completely.

4. Top each jar with 3 sprigs of dill and seal tightly.

5. Let the jars come to room temperature before placing them in the refrigerator.

6. Let chill and serve cold. Quick pickles can last for 3 to 4 months in the refrigerator.

dark chocolate—covered strawberries

(featured on That Season of Love Plate, page 130)

Spread the love with dark chocolate—covered strawberries. Savor the crunchy, sweet chocolate shell and the juicy strawberry beneath that's perfect for date night, ladies' night, or a snack just to treat yourself.

Makes 12 strawberries

1 pint fresh strawberries with stems

2 cups chopped dark chocolate or dark chocolate chips

½ cup chopped white chocolate or white chocolate chips, for drizzling

1. Gently wash and dry the strawberries and lay them out on a baking sheet lined with parchment paper. The strawberries must be completely dry before dipping.

2. Melt the dark chocolate in a microwave-safe bowl for 30 seconds. Stir and repeat once more until the chocolate is completely melted.

3. Holding the stem end, dip a strawberry into the melted chocolate, covering three-fourths of the fruit. Set it back on the baking sheet.

4. Repeat until all the strawberries are covered. Cover and place the baking sheet in the refrigerator until the chocolate cools and hardens, about 30 minutes.

5. Once the chocolate has hardened, repeat step 2 with the white chocolate.

6. Using a spoon, drizzle the white chocolate over the chilled strawberries in a sweeping motion.

7. Let the strawberries cool in the refrigerator for 10 more minutes before serving. They will stay fresh in the fridge for up to 2 days.

4

CARBS
ARE
YOUR
FRIEND

*Something magical happens when bread and cheese
come together. In France, most meals there start (and end)
with the simplicity of delicious fresh baked bread and an
assortment of French cheeses. While entertaining, food and
wine pairings are naturally considered, yet bread and cheese
pairings are just as important. You want to find a combination
that complements, but doesn't overwhelm the flavors of
either item. For me, baking is a mixture of comfort and
creativity. I love spending time in the kitchen preparing
delicious and beautiful things for those I love.*

—ELISA MARSHALL,
FOUNDER OF MAMAN BAKERY,
NEW YORK CITY AND TORONTO

Now that you've adorned your cheese and Salami River with colorful produce, it's time for step 4 in the Cheese By Numbers method: crunch. At this point, you'll notice that your cheese plate has some empty spaces. The technique is to fill in the gaps on the plate so that it looks full and abundant. One of the most important aspects of That Cheese Plate is gratitude to your guests and loved ones, and giving them a bountiful spread thanks them for sharing this meal with you.

The crunch portion of the method covers (you guessed it) everything crunchy, from mixed nuts to crackers, chocolate to crisp bread. You need a vehicle for the cheese, such as crackers or bread, as well as an extra textural element. Most crunchy items are a neutral color palette, which can be a nice contrast to the bright colors of the cheese, meat, and produce.

your go-to crunch guide

There are endless options for adding crunch to That Cheese Plate. Choose from nuts and seeds, crackers and bread, or even indulge in some decadent sweets. Use all of the crunch at once, in pairs, or on the plate solo. It's all about what moves you in the moment.

NUTS AND SEEDS

Nuts and seeds are an excellent source of protein and come in a wide variety of flavors and sizes. They're also the perfect way to fill in the small spaces on the plate while offering your guests something salty and crunchy to snack on. I like to use almonds, cashews, walnuts, and even trail mix on my plates. For those with nut allergies, pepitas or corn nuts are a good alternative.

CRACKERS AND BREAD

Crackers are useful for hard cheeses, and bread for soft, gooey cheeses. Feel free to branch out and get creative: if you're making a meze plate, go with some fresh pita bread. If you're cutting into a fresh burrata, toast up some baguette. Combining the various textures of cheese and crackers creates a sensory experience. To be honest, I could eat crackers and bread with every meal. Gluten is definitely self-care for me. Some of my favorites are flatbread crackers, seeded crackers, baguettes, and water crackers.

SNACKS

I love adding snacks of the crunchy, non-cracker variety to a cheese plate. If you're having a movie night, why not add some popcorn? Making a plate with savory dips? Add potato or tortilla chips. Have fun and use whatever snacks are in your pantry to set your cheese plate apart.

SWEETS

Sweets are a bit unconventional for a cheese plate, which makes them all the more fun. I love adding chocolate to a sweet plate, or cookies for the holidays. Sweet, crunchy items transform your plate with an added flavor element. My sweet tooth typically craves dark chocolate, hard candy, cookies, and shortbread.

an ode to
making sourdough bread

Sourdough is the oldest form of leavened bread, discovered when wild yeast accidentally drifted into dough mixes millennia ago. The fact that we can use natural bacteria in the air to ferment flour and water is a reminder that there is always life all around us, even if we can't see it. Sourdough bread making has recently developed a cult following, especially among my generation (millennials, I'm looking at you). It's a chance to slow down and discover the meditative art of baking, and it helps satisfy our urge to unplug from the Internet and connect to a tangible activity. Baking bread is the perfect opportunity for self-imposed offline time. It can take up to forty hours to make one loaf, teaching us that we don't always need the instant gratification of our tech-obsessed age. There are many parallels between cheese plate creation and bread making. Building a cheese plate requires the same attention to detail. When you work with your hands, it's easier to remain present. Just like aging meat and cheese, you can't speed up the natural process artificially. It takes time, patience, and reliance on the unseen. There's also something satisfying about such simple ingredients yielding impressive results. Now what happens when you put sourdough bread on a cheese plate? You achieve the perfect combination of two meditative (and delicious) activities.

that ESSENTIAL CRUNCH plate

This plate is the ultimate crunchy showcase,
featuring my favorite crackers and nuts to pair
with a delicious array of cheeses.

Key: The Plate: Square slate board, 12 × 12 inches

1: CHEESE

36-month-aged gouda

Cambozola (gorgonzola and camembert blend)

Oma (soft cow's milk cheese)

2: MEAT

Prosciutto

3: PRODUCE

Dried apricots

Concord grapes

4: CRUNCH

DIY Flatbread Crackers (recipe on page 179)

Seeded crackers

Gluten-free crackers

Mixed nuts

5: DIP

Caramelized onion jam

6: GARNISH

Dried strawflowers

Fresh rosemary

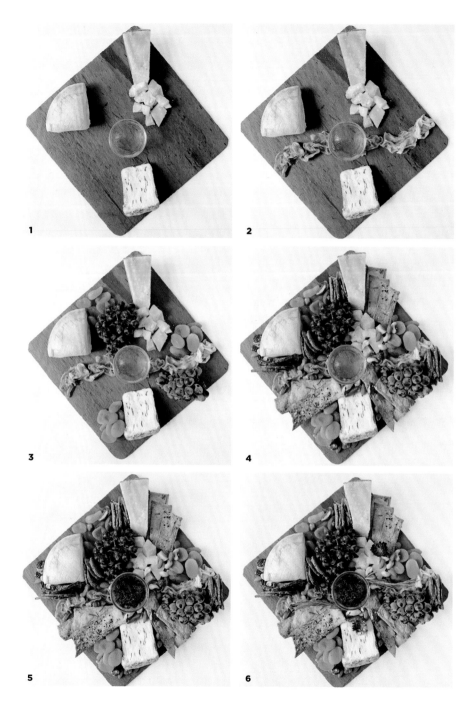

Rise and shine! What better way to start
the morning than with a bagel platter?

Key: The Plate: Rectangular wooden cutting board, 10 × 14 inches

1: CHEESE

French brie

Boursin

2: MEAT

Smoked salmon

Genoa salami

3: PRODUCE

Persian cucumbers

Capers

Red onions

Lemons

Blood oranges

Grapefruit

Castelvetrano olives

4: CRUNCH

Almonds

Flatbread crackers

Mini bagels

5: DIP

Fig jam

6: GARNISH

*Yellow and white mini
roses*

Fresh dill

Fresh rosemary

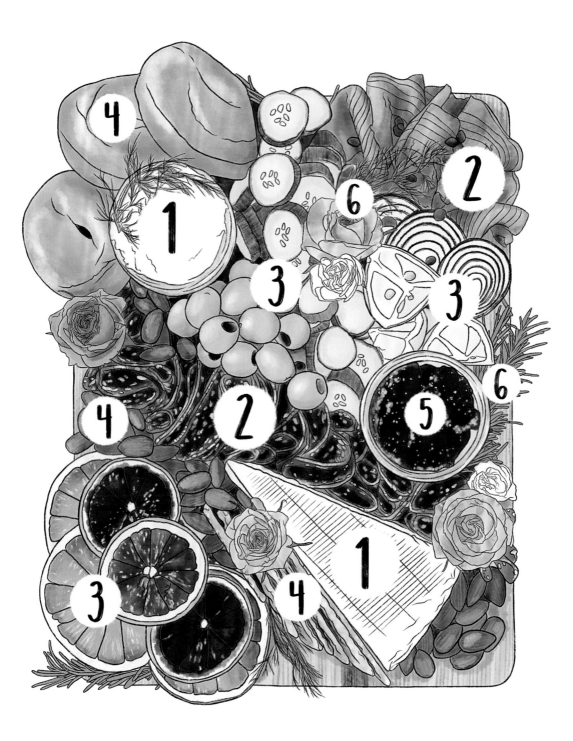

that DECONSTRUCTED PIZZA plate

Transform a classic pizza parlor staple
into a unique cheese plate creation.
#TeamPineapplePizza forever.

Key: The Plate: Round soapstone with brass handles, 12-inch diameter

---

1: CHEESE

*Mozzarella slices
(layered with basil)*

Pecorino Toscano

2: MEAT

Prosciutto di Parma

Genoa salami

3: PRODUCE

*Grape tomatoes
(red and green)*

Fresh pineapple cubes

4: CRUNCH

French baguette

5: DIP

N/A

6: GARNISH

Fresh oregano

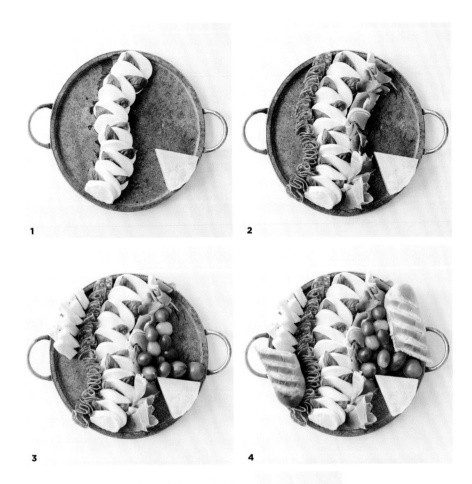

This is a bright and crunchy cheese plate
for the summertime. Chill by the pool and
snack on this board.

Key: The Plate: Round wooden board with handle, 10-inch diameter

---

1: CHEESE
Sharp cheddar
Gruyère

2: MEAT
N/A

3: PRODUCE
Rainier cherries
Strawberries
Peaches
Fresh apricots

4: CRUNCH
Flatbread crackers
Walnuts
Pistachios

5: DIP
Red pepper jam

6: GARNISH
Yellow pansies
Tea roses

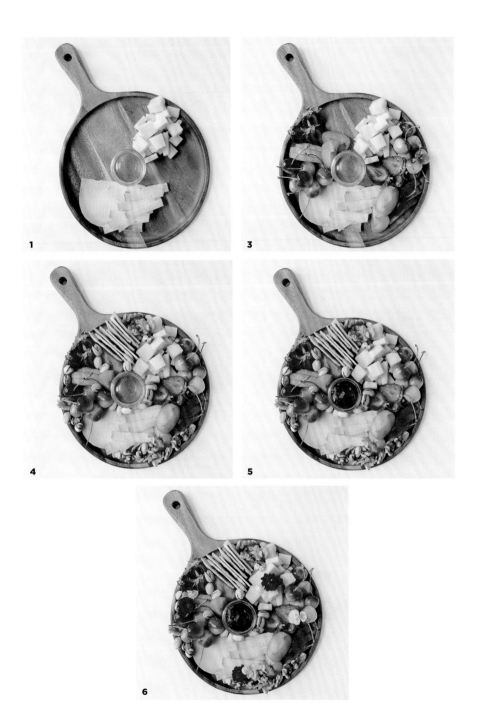

that BURRATA BAR plate

Choose your own burrata adventure. With a variety
of pairings, you and your guests can create your own
custom crostini with this plate.

Key: The Plate: Round wooden lazy Susan, 15-inch diameter

1: CHEESE

Burrata (2 balls)

2: MEAT

Prosciutto di Parma

Coppa

3: PRODUCE

Red radishes

Marinated artichokes

Fresh figs

Green olives

*Orange Peppadew
peppers*

*Grape tomatoes
(red and yellow)*

Green grapes

4: CRUNCH

Toasted bread

Taralli *crackers
(Italian oval crackers)*

Parmesan crisps

5: DIP

Balsamic glaze

6: GARNISH

Fresh basil

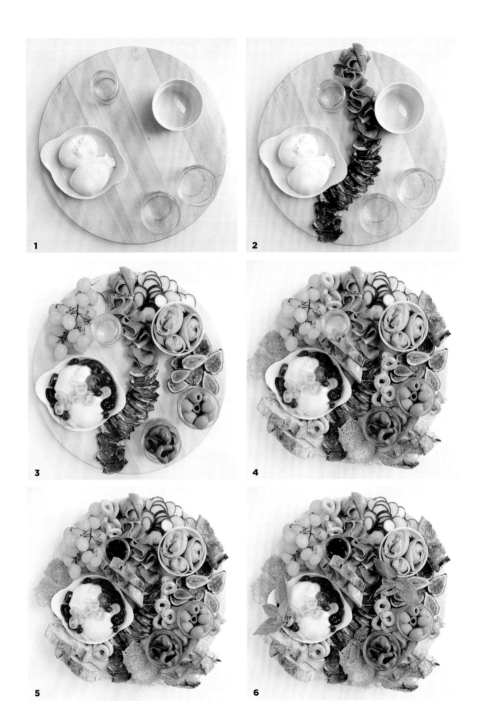

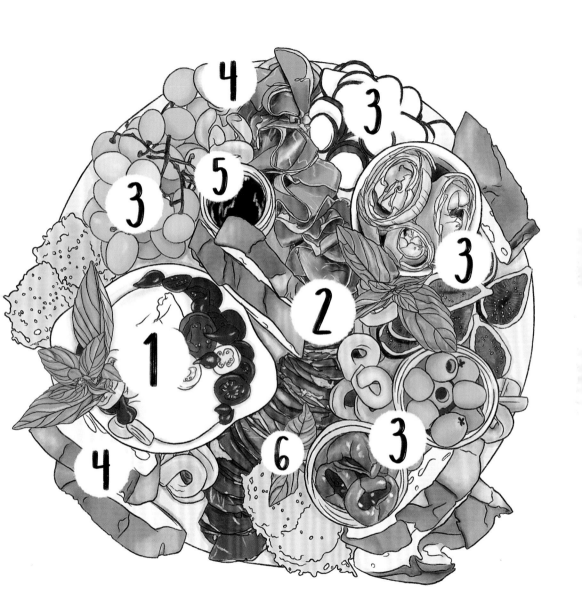

that TREAT YOURSELF plate

Everyone loves a good candy binge,
so we're putting the treat in "trick or treat"
with this plate.

Key: The Plate: Rectangular wooden board, 9½ × 13½ inches

1: CHEESE

Triple crème brie

Manchego

2: MEAT

Hard salami

3: PRODUCE

Fresh figs

Gala apples

Red grapes

4: CRUNCH

Dark chocolate peanut-butter cups

Unsalted mixed nuts

Leaf-shaped sugar cookies

Red licorice

Milk chocolate bars

5: DIP

Quince jam

6: GARNISH

Blue thistle flowers

Fresh rosemary

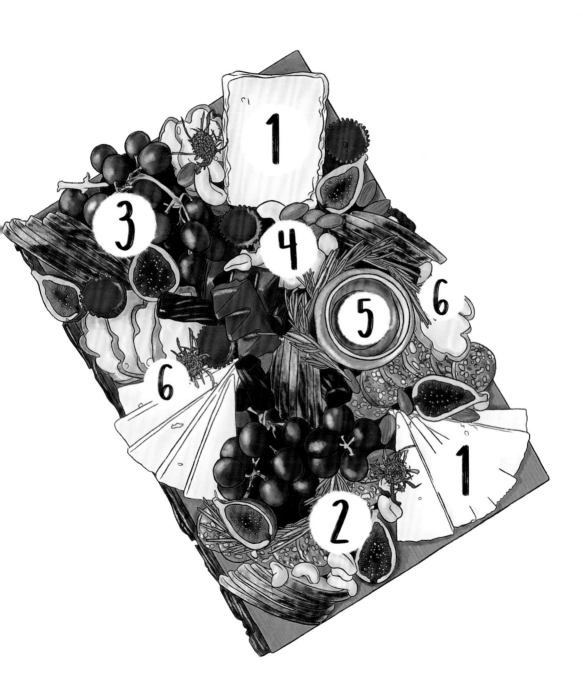

Feeling a bit on the sweeter side today?
This plate features crunchy shortbread cookies,
decadent dark chocolate, and salty Marcona almonds.

··
Key: The Plate: Round slate board, 12-inch diameter
··

1: CHEESE

Camembert

2: MEAT

N/A

3: PRODUCE

Strawberries

Gala apples

Fresh figs

4: CRUNCH

Dark chocolate

Marcona almonds

Thin, crisp crackers

Shortbread cookies

5: DIP

Fresh honeycomb

6: GARNISH

Fresh thyme

Pink carnations

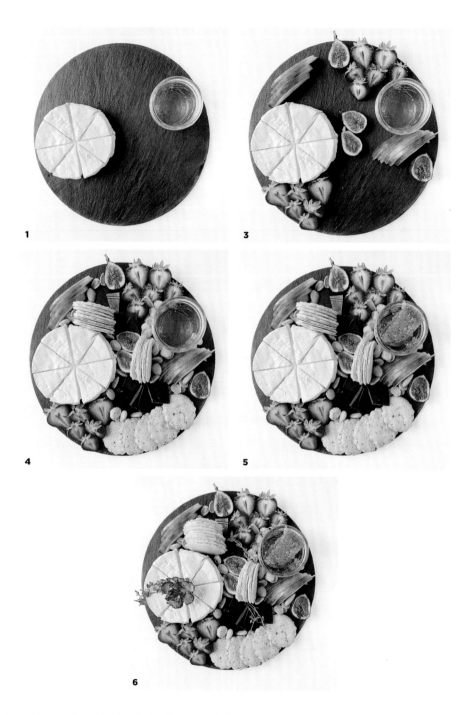

diy flatbread crackers

(featured on That Essential Crunch Plate, page 150)

Impress your guests with an incredibly simple do-it-yourself cracker recipe (not to mention, kneading dough is a fantastic stress reliever!).

Makes 30 crackers

1½ cups all-purpose flour, plus more for dusting

1½ teaspoons kosher salt

1 teaspoon sugar

¼ cup freshly grated Parmigiano-Reggiano

2 tablespoons rosemary leaves, divided

½ cup cold water

3 tablespoons extra-virgin olive oil

Coarse sea salt, for garnish (option to add other spices as well)

1. Preheat the oven to 400°F and line a baking sheet with parchment paper.

2. In a medium mixing bowl, combine the flour, Kosher salt, sugar, and cheese. Chop 1 tablespoon of the rosemary and stir it in with the olive oil, and ½ cup cold water. Stir until the mixture comes together as a sticky dough, about 4 minutes.

3. Transfer the dough to a lightly floured surface and knead for 2 minutes, until it no longer sticks to the surface. Cut the dough in half.

4. Roll out one half to a ⅛-inch thickness. Brush lightly with water and sprinkle with coarse sea salt and preferred seasoning (I used "Everything Bagel" seasoning). Repeat with the other half.

5. Cut each half into 2 × 5-inch rectangles. With lightly floured fingers, transfer the rectangles to the prepared baking sheet.

6. Bake for 10 to 12 minutes, until browned and crunchy. Let fully cool and harden before serving, garnishing with the remaining rosemary. These crackers will last for up to 3 days stored in an airtight container.

5
S P R E A D
T H E
L O V E

I've always considered honey one of nature's most unique and wonderful foods. It captures and relays the unique flavors of a place and environment as well as anything. When I travel, I collect honey from that region. Each honey contains the flavor notes of the flowers where those bees were collecting nectar. One spoonful instantly transports me back to that place. It's a wonderful way to reflect on past travel experiences. Today I'm grateful to be producing and distributing a food product, something physical that can't be downloaded from the Internet.

—MIKE KURTZ,
FOUNDER OF MIKE'S HOT HONEY

Now it's time for step 5 of the Cheese By Numbers method. Fill up those empty ramekins with an array of sweet and savory dips and spreads. Whether smeared on a cracker with cheese or dolloped on veggies, dips are the perfect addition to a cheese plate, providing an array of robust flavors and colors. Stick with a classic dip like fig jam, or be a bit more adventurous and mix things up with hummus or spicy honey. Dips add an extra textural element to the plate to engage our sense of touch and taste. They can also help set the flavor theme for your cheese plate. Use salsa for a Mexican plate, or tzatziki for a Greek-inspired plate. Store-bought or homemade, dips add some extra variety and pizzazz to your creation.

sweet dips:
a perfect pairing

Cheese pairs wonderfully with sweet dips like jam, compote, and honey, which act as a balance to its savory flavor profile. But how do you choose the right jam for your cheese? First, consider the cheese's age. Fresh or soft cheeses are naturally a bit sweeter, while aged cheeses have a stronger, denser flavor. For example, a sharp cheddar pairs nicely with something on the sweeter end of the spectrum, like apple jam. A spicy blue cheese goes well with black currant jam. The sweet acidic bite of the currant cuts through the rich texture of the cheese, while the creaminess neutralizes your palate. Here are some other suggested tasty cheese and jam pairings. Keep in mind, pairings are personal, and there's no right or wrong—follow your taste buds and have fun with it.

savory dips:
the life of the party

Savory dips are an easy and approachable starter snack. Putting savory dips on a cheese plate brings the appetizer game to a whole new level. They're the ultimate social connector at any gathering. You may notice that people tend to gravitate toward the dip. (And who knows, maybe one day you'll meet your future partner by accidentally bumping hands while dipping into the guacamole at a party. . . .) Some savory dips I love to mix up on my cheese plates are fondue cheese, hummus, mustard, pimento dip, queso, spicy honey, and salsa.

that HOT HONEY plate

I'm addicted to spicy honey, and I put it
on everything, so I created this ode to
this sweet, hot favorite.

Key: The Plate: Round wooden board with handle, 10-inch diameter

1: CHEESE
Asiago
Blue

2: MEAT
Soppressata, sliced

3: PRODUCE
*Mini sweet peppers
(yellow, orange,
and red)*
*Baby carrots (yellow
and orange)*
Grape tomatoes

4: CRUNCH
Spiced almonds
Turmeric crackers
Pistachios

5: DIP
Spicy honey

6: GARNISH
Fresh rosemary

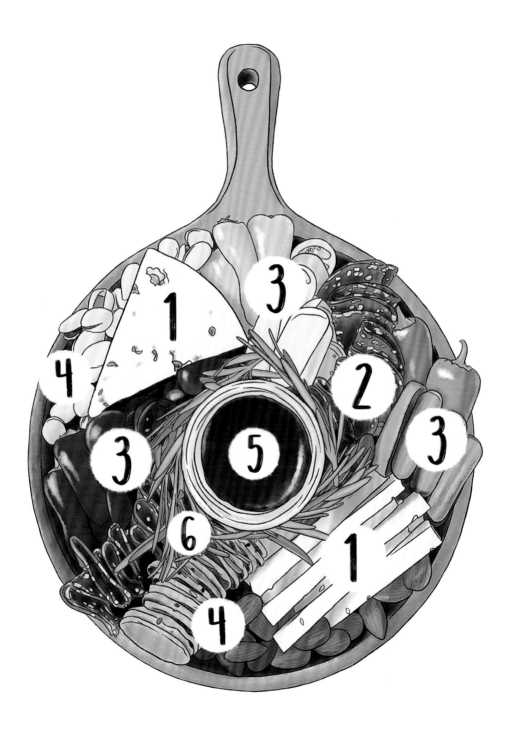

that MEZE PLATTER plate

It's a pita party. Dive into this take on a meze platter, complete with fresh feta, tzatziki, and creamy hummus.

Key: The Plate: Round wooden board, 15-inch diameter

1: CHEESE

Fresh feta

2: MEAT

N/A

3: PRODUCE

Persian cucumbers

Red radishes (some whole with stem and leaves, some sliced)

Green olives

Grape tomatoes (red and yellow)

4: CRUNCH

Pita chips

Baked pita bread

5: DIP

Tzatziki

Marissa's Homemade Hummus (recipe on page 223)

6: GARNISH

Fresh parsley

Fresh dill

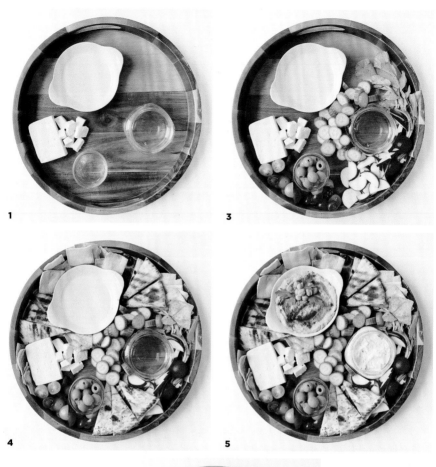

that QUESO AND GUAC plate

I love this colorful fiesta plate—perfect to pair with a margarita (and I don't charge extra for guac!).

Key: The Plate: Round soapstone with brass handles, 12-inch diameter

---

1: CHEESE
Pepper Jack

2: MEAT
Chorizo

3: PRODUCE
Fresh jalapeños

Red radishes

Grape tomatoes (red and yellow)

Mini sweet peppers (orange, yellow, and red)

Limes

4: CRUNCH
Marcona almonds

Tortilla chips

5: DIP
Queso

Guacamole

6: GARNISH
Zinnias

Fresh cilantro

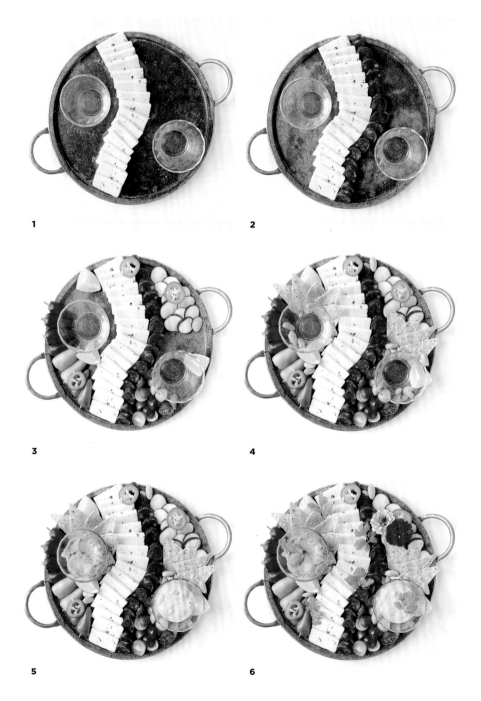

1

2

3

4

5

6

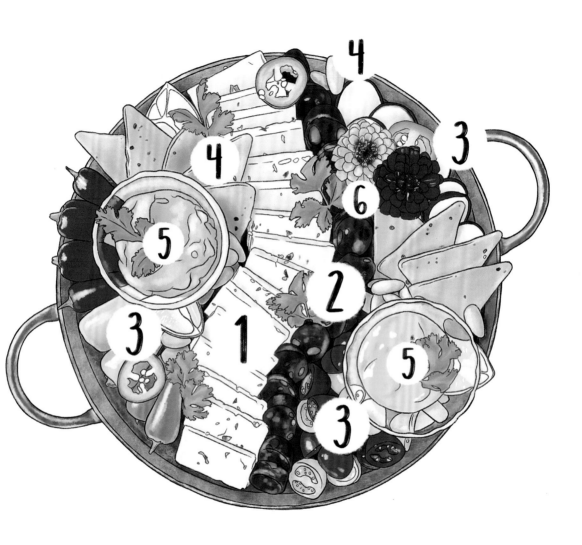

that PIMENTO PARTY plate

Pimento cheese is a staple in Southern cooking and
perfect for your summer gatherings. Pour some sweet tea
and spread that pimento cheese on a crisp cracker.

Key: The Plate: Rectangular plastic tray, 10 × 15 inches

1: CHEESE

Sharp cheddar

2: MEAT

Genoa salami, sliced

3: PRODUCE

Peaches

Celery

*Grape tomatoes (red
and yellow)*

Persian cucumbers

4: CRUNCH

Wheat crackers

Almonds

Water crackers

Butter crackers

5: DIP

*Southern Pimento
Cheese (recipe on
page 224)*

6: GARNISH

Fresh chives

*Baby's breath (remove
before consumption)*

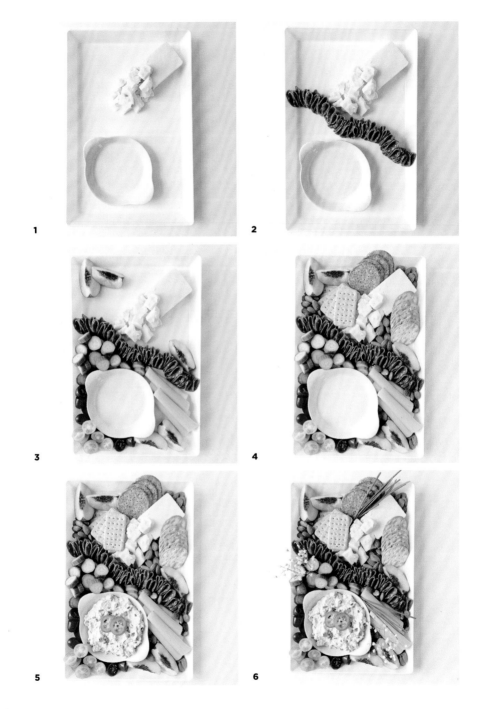

SWEET LITTLE PARM *plate*

If you've been eating grated parmesan from a plastic container,
you're doing it wrong. Let the flavor of Parmigiano-Reggiano shine
on this autumnal plate with a sweet honey to pair.

Key: The Plate: Round porcelain dinner plate, 12-inch diameter

1: CHEESE
*White Gold
Parmigiano-Reggiano*

2: MEAT
Prosciutto di Parma

3: PRODUCE
*Dried apricots
Dried cherries
Dried figs*

4: CRUNCH
*Almonds
Flatbread crackers*

5: DIP
Organic honey

6: GARNISH
*Dried strawflowers
Fresh rosemary
Dried lily petals*

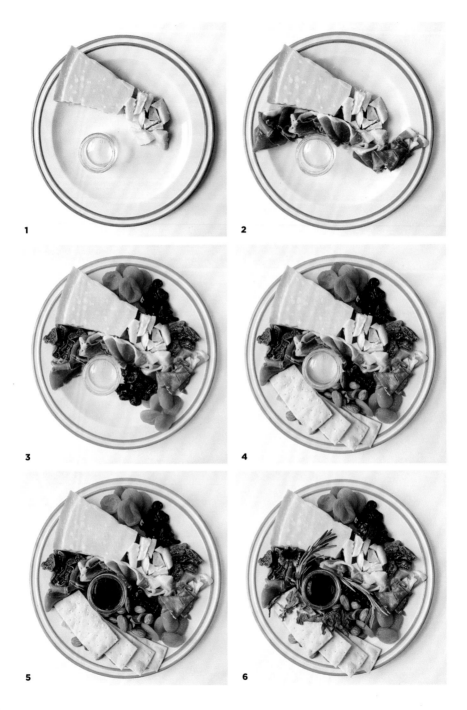

that BERRY-PICKING plate

This plate will make you feel as if you just picked a basket of fresh berries from a bountiful garden, turned on your stove, and boiled them into jam. Maybe you did do that. If so, good for you.

Key: The Plate: Rectangular wooden board, 11 × 17 inches

1: CHEESE
French brie
Sharp cheddar

2: MEAT
Prosciutto

3: PRODUCE
Blueberries
Blackberries
Raspberries

4: CRUNCH
Walnuts
Flatbread crackers

5: DIP
Raspberry jam
Cherry compote
Strawberry rhubarb jam

6: GARNISH
Pansies
Dried strawflowers

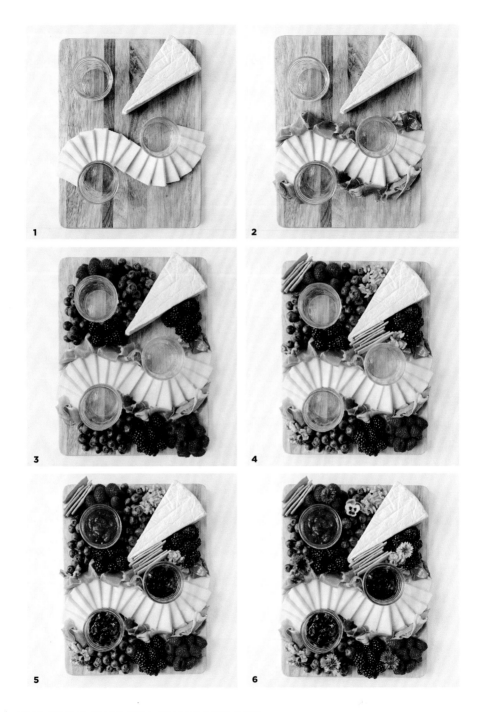

I think the best part about skiing is eating afterward.
Even if you don't ski, this decadent fondue will warm you up after
spending time out in the cold weather.

Key: The Plate: Rectangular wooden board, 9½ × 13½ inches

1: CHEESE
Gruyère

2: MEAT
Capocollo

3: PRODUCE
Red radishes
Green grapes

Gala apples
Fresh figs
Anjou pears
Purple grapes
Broccoli

4: CRUNCH
Bread cubes
Cheese twists

Mixed nuts
Waffle cookies

5: DIP
Cheese fondue

6: GARNISH
Fresh rosemary
Fresh thyme

TANGY TASTE plate

This is a plate for our tangy fans out there.
Pair crunchy pickles with a trio of mustards.
Bonus points: Soft pretzels!

Key: The Plate: Round wooden lazy Susan, 15-inch diameter

1: CHEESE
Taleggio
Blue
Sharp cheddar

2: MEAT
Hard salami

3: PRODUCE
Red radishes
Cornichons
Castelvetrano olives
Marinated artichokes

4: CRUNCH
Mixed nuts
Pistachios
Pretzels
Soft pretzels

5: DIP
Whole-grain mustard
Honey mustard
Dijon mustard

6: GARNISH
Fresh rosemary
Dried globe amaranth flowers

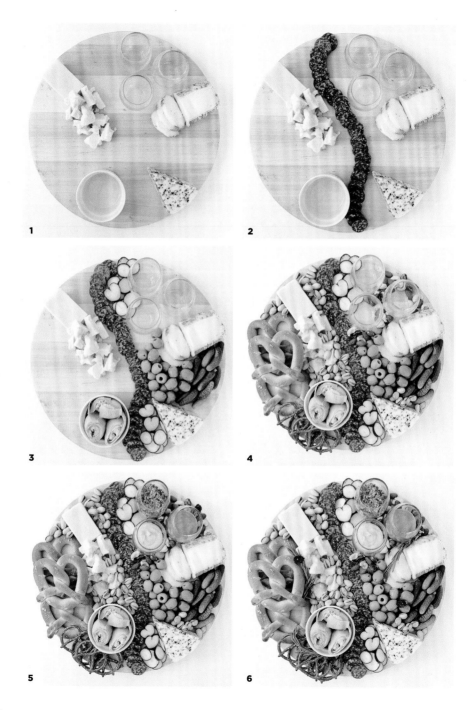

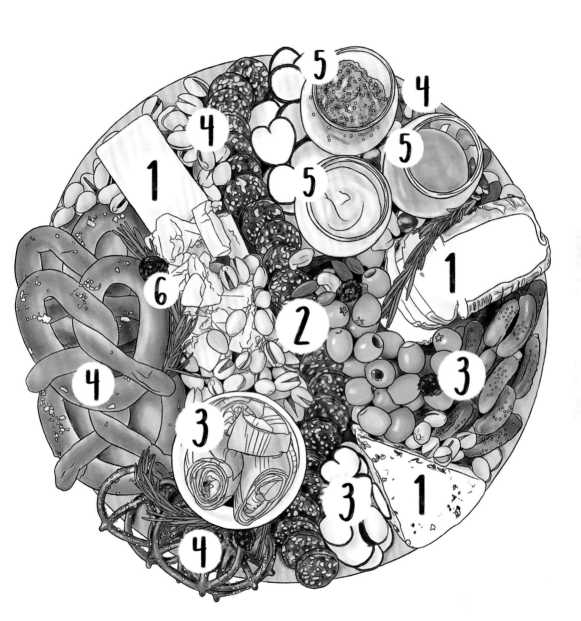

that MORNING MARMALADE plate

Wake up to a breakfast board with
sweet marmalade paired with the very delicious
yet very underrated cottage cheese.

Key: The Plate: Round porcelain plate, 11-inch diameter

1: CHEESE

5-year-aged gouda

Cottage cheese

2: MEAT

Chicken apple sausage

3: PRODUCE

Champagne grapes

Strawberries

Honeydew melon

Cantaloupe

4: CRUNCH

Toasted English muffins

Mixed nuts

5: DIP

Orange marmalade

Apricot jam

6: GARNISH

Zinnias

Fresh sage

Nasturtiums

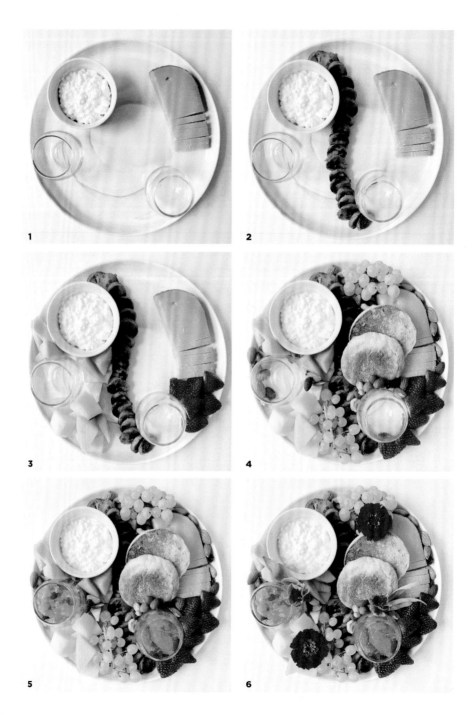

marissa's homemade hummus

(featured on That Meze Platter Plate, page 190)

One of my very first purchases in New York City was a food processor, and, though I could hardly fit it in my tiny kitchen cabinets, I've never looked back. My goal: the perfect homemade hummus, with five simple ingredients and added spices. You can dip anything into hummus and it'll taste delicious. That's my rule.

Makes 2 cups

1 (15-ounce) can chickpeas, drained, a few set aside for garnish

2 garlic cloves, sliced

1 tablespoon tahini

Juice of ½ lemon

1 teaspoon ground cumin

3 tablespoons extra-virgin olive oil, plus more as needed

Kosher salt and freshly ground black pepper to taste

Paprika, for garnish

Parsley, for garnish

1. In a food processor, combine the chickpeas, garlic, tahini, lemon juice, cumin, and olive oil. Blend until smooth. If the consistency is too thick, add more olive oil as needed.

2. Add salt and pepper to taste.

3. Spoon the hummus into a serving dish and garnish with a drizzle of olive oil, a few chickpeas, and a dash of paprika and chopped parsley. The hummus can be refrigerated in an airtight container for 3 to 4 days.

southern pimento cheese

(featured on That Pimento Party Plate, page 198)

Pimento cheese is quintessential Southern cuisine. A warning, though: This creamy, slightly sweet and spicy spread is totally addictive. Spread it on crackers, chips, or vegetables—pimento cheese goes well with just about everything.

Makes 2 cups

2 cups or 8 ounces grated extra-sharp cheddar

8 ounces cream cheese, softened

½ cup mayonnaise

¼ teaspoon garlic powder

¼ teaspoon cayenne pepper

¼ teaspoon onion powder

1 jalapeño, seeded and minced

1 (4-ounce) jar diced pimentos, drained

Kosher salt and freshly ground black pepper

Sliced and chopped jalapeños for garnish

Chopped chives for garnish

1. In a medium bowl, combine the cheddar, cream cheese, mayonnaise, garlic powder, cayenne, and onion powder. Mix well until all the items are blended together.

2. Fold in the jalapeño and pimentos until thoroughly combined.

3. Season with salt and black pepper to taste. Garnish with jalapeños and chives and serve. Pimento cheese will keep in the refrigerator up to a week.

6

THYME
TO
SHINE

*In our restaurants, our chief focus is on the graciousness of our
service and the deliciousness of our food. But I'd be remiss not
to acknowledge the importance of aesthetics, whether it is the
way the room makes you feel when you step through the doors
or the way the food looks on the plate when it is placed in front of
you. The first impression of any dish happens when you look at
it; the more thoughtfully it is presented, the more likely you will
be to enjoy that first bite. So put a little energy into not only what
you are serving but how you're serving it. It goes a long way.*

—WILL GUIDARA,
AMERICAN RESTAURATEUR

And now step 6, the grand finale, the "om" at the end of your practice. The
garnish acts as the proverbial cherry on top of your cheese plate creation.
After going through the Cheese By Numbers method, we end with this special aesthetic addition. I've heard that it takes only seven seconds to make
a first impression, and that can definitely apply to your cheese plate. Simple
decorative elements like fresh herbs and edible flowers can make all the dif-
ference and set your plate apart. The garnish teaches us to pay attention to
details, those little things that spark joy, while transforming your cheese
plate into a true work of art.

herbs

Fresh herbs make a perfect garnish to elevate your cheese plate, adding an aromatic touch and incorporating an earthy element. I love using fresh rosemary all year round, but especially during the winter. Rosemary sprigs resemble pine trees and smell like a savory feast roasting in the oven. You can also incorporate fresh herbs like thyme, sage, parsley, oregano, basil, and mint. In addition to their looks and aroma, herbs add a depth of flavor to cheese pairings as well. I love pairing feta with fresh parsley, and mozzarella with fresh basil.

flowers

Flowers add a lovely, delicate, and colorful element to your plate, but always make sure your blooms are edible and food-safe if you plan on eating them. True edible flowers can sometimes be hard to track down, but I've been able to find them in the produce section of my grocery store, at farmers' markets, and online. If you're lucky enough to have a garden, grow your own garnish! Pansies, lavender, lilies, carnations, daisies, and roses are all easy to grow and, believe it or not, completely edible.

other flair

Sometimes, if I'm building a themed plate, I'll decorate with some unconventional items. For example, you can decorate your cheese plate with mini paper umbrellas for a tropical theme, or use a small pumpkin for an autumnal theme. Get weird, get wacky, get creative. Just remember to remove them before eating!

that GARDEN plate

Garnished with vibrant edible flowers
from the garden, this is the perfect plate
for a spring picnic.

Key: The Plate: Round soapstone with brass handles, 12-inch diameter

1: CHEESE

Goat brie

Midnight Moon
(goat gouda)

2: MEAT

Speck

3: PRODUCE

Sugar snap peas

Raspberries

Grapefruit

Concord grapes

4: CRUNCH

Flatbread crackers

Almonds

Fruit and nut crackers

5: DIP

Orange marmalade

6: GARNISH

Butterfly pea flowers

Fresh rosemary

Zinnias

Nasturtiums

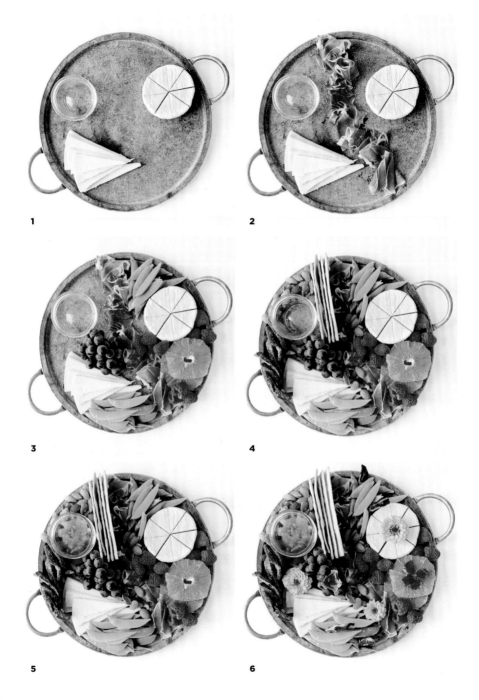

1

2

3

4

5

6

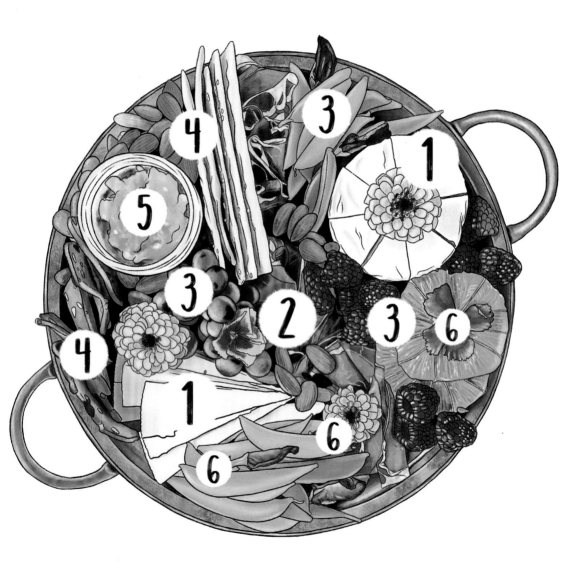

FRESH HERBS plate

You'll be able to smell this plate a mile away
thanks to the array of aromatic herbs—
so fresh and so green.

Key: The Plate: Round slate board, 12-inch diameter

1: CHEESE

Keep Dreaming (cow's milk camembert)

Comté

2: MEAT

Genoa salami

3: PRODUCE

Strawberries

Broccoli

Sugar snap peas

Green bell peppers

4: CRUNCH

Pepitas

5: DIP

Organic honey

6: GARNISH

Fresh rosemary

Fresh sage

Fresh mint

Fresh thyme

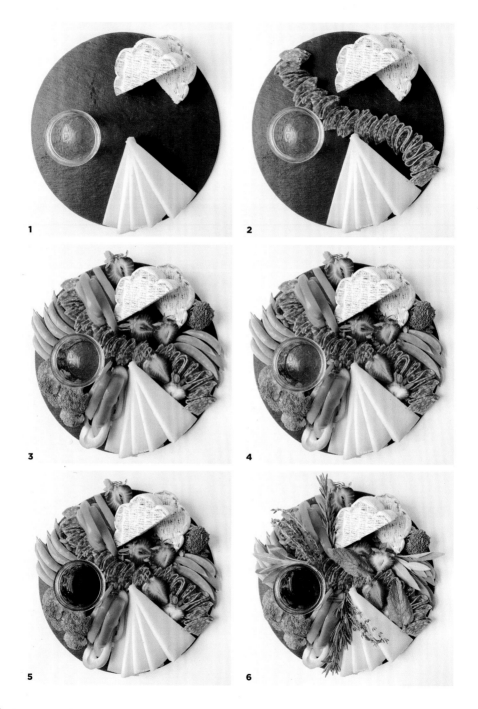

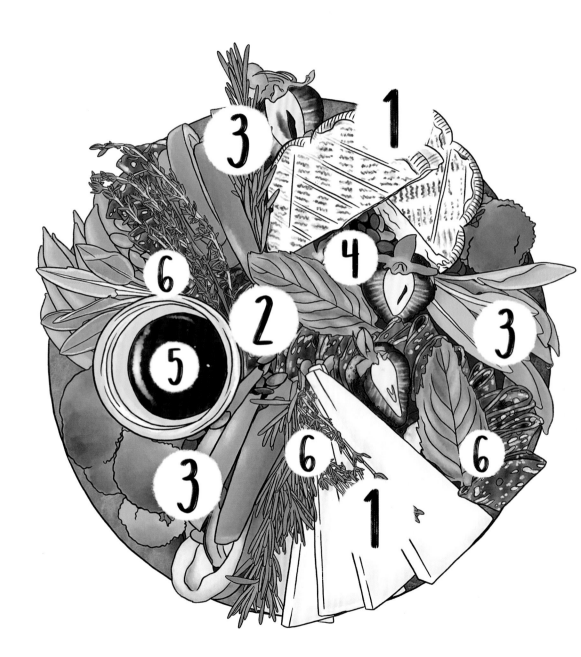

BASIL AND BLOOMS *plate*

Feel the breeze and smell the flowers.
This plate captures the vibrant essence of summer.

1: CHEESE

Mini mozzarella balls

Fresh feta

2: MEAT

Prosciutto

3: PRODUCE

*Cherry tomatoes
(red and orange)*

Persian cucumbers

Castelvetrano olives

4: CRUNCH

Pistachios

Flatbread crackers

5: DIP

Strawberry rhubarb jam

6: GARNISH

Fresh basil

Pink carnations

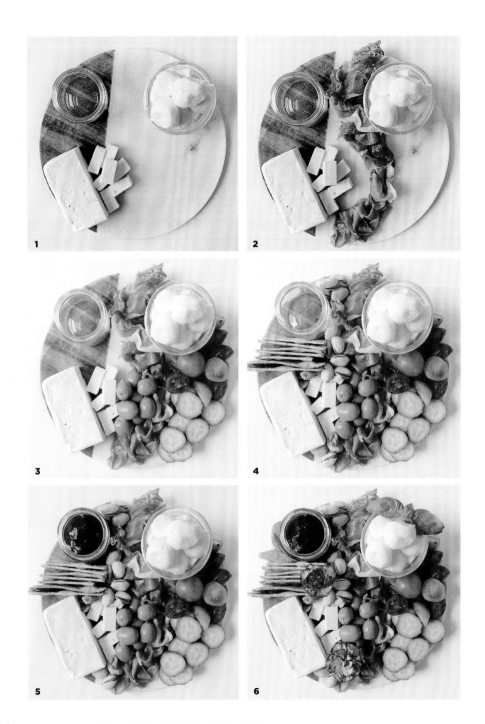

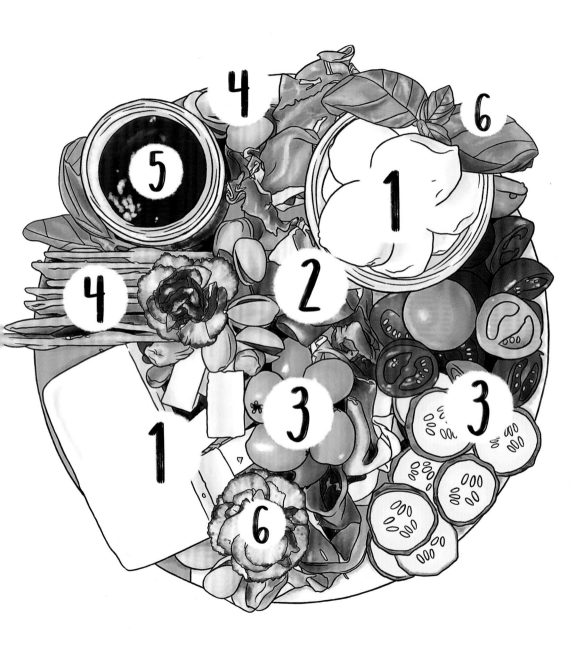

With only one cheese, you can make this plate for
less than thirty dollars using ingredients from the grocery store!
Garnish with herbs to class it up.

Key: The Plate: Round porcelain plate, 11-inch diameter

1: CHEESE
Gruyère

2: MEAT
Genoa salami, sliced

3: PRODUCE
Blackberries
Strawberries
Blueberries

4: CRUNCH
Mixed nuts
Butter crackers

5: DIP
Raspberry jam

6: GARNISH
Fresh thyme

that
LAVENDER
FIELDS
plate

Blending floral notes with fresh cheese
complexities, this lavender plate
smells and tastes like a dream.

Key: The Plate: Round wooden board with handle, 10-inch diameter

1: CHEESE

Humboldt Fog (soft-ripened goat cheese)

Ossau-Iraty

2: MEAT

N/A

3: PRODUCE

Blackberries

Persian cucumbers

Blueberries

4: CRUNCH

Almonds

Fresh sourdough bread

5: DIP

Red currant jam

6: GARNISH

Fresh lavender

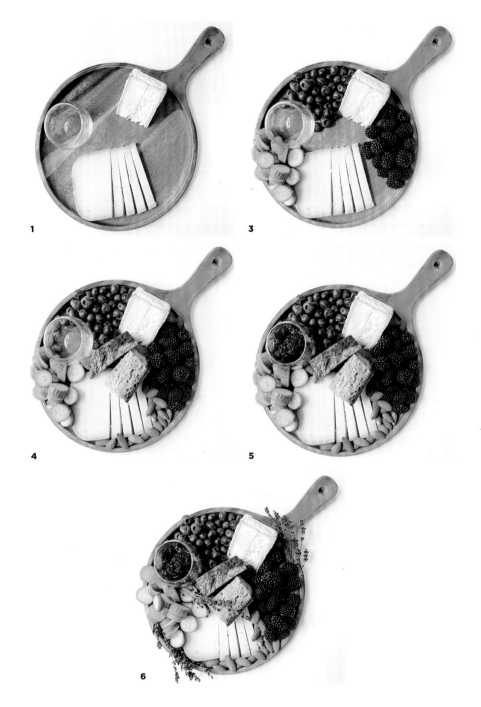

that GROW YOUR OWN GARNISH plate

Beautify your plate with an array
of edible herbs and flowers you can grow in
your own garden!

Key: The Plate: Rectangular wooden cutting board, 10 × 14 inches

1: CHEESE

Grand Cru (swiss-style
cow's milk cheese)

Havarti

2: MEAT

Genoa salami, sliced

3: PRODUCE

Strawberries

Rainier cherries

Peaches

Blueberries

4: CRUNCH

Pistachios

Butter crackers

5: DIP

Organic honey

6: GARNISH

Yellow and purple
pansies

Borage

Fresh thyme

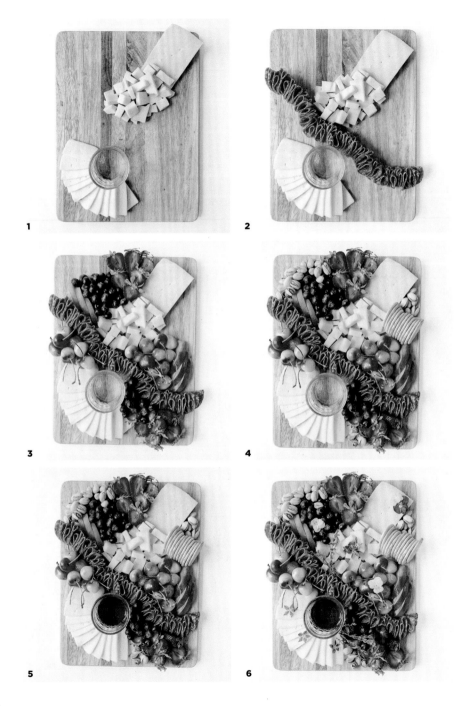

1

2

3

4

5

6

IT'S YOUR BIRTHDAY *that plate*

What better way to celebrate a birthday
than with a cake made entirely of cheese.
Your wish has been granted!

Key: The Plate: Round marble plate, 8-inch diameter

1: CHEESE

1 (4-inch) wheel
Humboldt Fog
(soft-ripened
goat cheese)

1 (3-inch) wheel
goat brie

2: MEAT

Prosciutto

3: PRODUCE

Fresh figs

Raspberries

Blueberries

4: CRUNCH

Mixed nuts

5: DIP

Drizzled honey

6: GARNISH

Fresh thyme

Pink carnations

2 birthday candles
(Make a wish!)

FOLIAGE plate

Pumpkin spice is in the air and the leaves are changing.
Get into the autumnal mood with this plate,
garnished with assorted dried flowers.

Key: The Plate: Rectangular wooden board, 9½ × 13½ inches

1: CHEESE

Cambozola

Mimolette

2: MEAT

Fig salami

3: PRODUCE

Concord grapes

Dried apricots

Gala apples

Raspberries

4: CRUNCH

Mixed nuts

Seeded crackers

5: DIP

Caramelized onion jam

6: GARNISH

Dried strawflowers

Dried lily petals

that bonus content

a cheese pairing for your star sign

On my twenty-sixth birthday, I saw an astrologist as a gift to myself. By providing her with only the date, time, and location of my birth, she read my chart and literally peered into my soul, describing my personality with spooky accuracy. Just like cheese, we are all very complex and unique. Naturally, I decided to give each zodiac sign its own cheese pairing too.

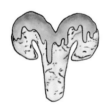

ARIES (March 21–April 19): Aries are passionate, motivated, and confident. Those born under this sign lead with blind optimism and self-determination.

ARIES CHEESE PAIRING: Strong blue cheese with spicy honey—a pungent blue with a fiery kick.

TAURUS (April 20–May 20): Reliable and patient, Tauruses love cooking and the luxuries in life. Those born under this earth sign are grounded and practical, and they appreciate the beauty of the material world.

TAURUS CHEESE PAIRING: Harbison, a decadent camembert, with a crisp baguette. Nothing better than velvety, earthy cheese on freshly baked bread.

GEMINI (May 21–June 20): Quick and witty, Geminis have a knack for communication and are always full of ideas. Those born under this air sign are known to have a "split personality"—they can adapt to any situation thrown their way.

GEMINI CHEESE PAIRING: Sharp gruyère, studded with tyrosine crystals, and fig jam—two opposing salty and sweet flavors with an unexpected crunch to keep you on your toes.

CANCER (June 21–July 22): Emotional, imaginative, and sympathetic, Cancers love a good meal with friends and spending time at home.

CANCER CHEESE PAIRING: Fresh feta and watermelon— a summertime snack to enjoy in the backyard at home.

LEO (July 23–August 22): Leos are creative, passionate, and cheerful, and love admiration. Those born under this fire sign are not afraid to be the center of attention and make for natural-born leaders.

LEO CHEESE PAIRING: Aged Pecorino Toscano and prosciutto, a popular and timeless pairing with a sharp bite and a salty finish.

VIRGO (August 23–September 22): Virgos are loyal, practical, kind, and hardworking. They enjoy books, nature, and organization.

VIRGO CHEESE PAIRING: Humboldt Fog and fresh figs. This goat cheese is light and easy, with some hidden complexities.

LIBRA (September 23–October 22): Libras are social, gracious, balanced, and cooperative. They enjoy harmony, relationships, and the outdoors. LIBRA CHEESE PAIRING: Cheese fondue with an assortment of items to dip. Libras love to share and can't decide on just one pairing.

SCORPIO (October 23–November 21): Scorpios are resourceful, determined, and a bit mysterious. They enjoy loyal friendships and grand passions. SCORPIO CHEESE PAIRING: Gouda and dark chocolate, a decadent duo with some unexpected tasting notes.

SAGITTARIUS (November 22–December 21): Sagittarians are generous, idealistic, and love to travel. They appreciate freedom, philosophy, and learning about different cultures. SAGITTARIUS CHEESE PAIRING: Mozzarella di Bufala with roasted tomatoes and basil—transport your taste buds to the Italian countryside.

CAPRICORN (December 22–January 19): Capricorns are responsible, disciplined hard workers. They enjoy tradition and family, and have the ability to lead the way. CAPRICORN CHEESE PAIRING: Cheddar and apples, a reliable and respected pairing that has stood the test of time.

AQUARIUS (January 20–February 18): Aquarians are original, independent, and love to help others. They are always trying to see the bigger picture and are natural humanitarians.

AQUARIUS CHEESE PAIRING: Coupole (soft-ripened goat cheese) and fresh berries—a quirky cheese with an approachable taste.

PISCES (February 19–March 20): Pisces are compassionate, artistic, and wise. They enjoy music, independence, and daydreaming.

PISCES CHEESE PAIRING: Comté and honey—a complex cheese with a sweet pairing that will keep your head in the clouds.

the art of the grazing table

If you're having a big party or just want to think outside the board, you can build directly on a countertop or flat surface: voilà, the grazing table. The key to the perfect grazing table is to utilize bowls, plates, or ramekins to set your foundation. Because there is more room to build upon, you want to somehow visualize the shape of your creation. Follow the Cheese By Numbers method, but make sure you have enough supplies. Grazing tables require a lot of food and prep time. I love decorating different elements of the table to create more detail and color. Add some arugula as a bed for different cheeses, and garnish any dips with herbs and edible flowers. I built this grazing table on a 6-foot table that I covered with butcher's paper. Don't be afraid to get creative!

1

2

3

4

1—CHEESE

Mozzarella with sliced cherry tomatoes

Cheddar

Labneh with herbs

Feta

2—MEAT

Genoa salami

Chorizo

Prosciutto-wrapped peaches and cantaloupe

3—PRODUCE

Mixed olives

Green olives

Grape leaves

Sugar snap peas

Red radishes

Raspberries

Blueberries

Fresh apricots

Persian cucumbers

4—CRUNCH

Pita bread

Almonds

Shelled pistachios

Sliced bread

5—DIP

Hummus with pine nuts

Tzatziki

6—GARNISH

Pansies

Tea roses

Borage

Fresh rosemary

Fresh basil

a plate for
every season

Cheese plates are a perennial favorite. Depending on the time of year, you can add a certain flair to set each plate apart. There is a cheese plate for every occasion. Here is a handy season-by-season guide to help.

spring

summer

coming full circle

Congrats! You've made That Cheese Plate in your own unique and beautiful way.

The Cheese By Numbers method gives you the chance to ground yourself, to indulge your soul (and your appetite), and to celebrate your passion for cheese. It's self-care at its very best. You can relax your way into entertaining, and then focus on the best part: eating it!

Enjoy your beautiful creation. The plate was made to be destroyed, so feel the cathartic release of digging into your work of art, tasting the gooey cheese and savory pairings. Most important, enjoy those around you. Hosting a gathering lets you bring people together to share a wonderful experience. It's a time to reflect, decompress, and indulge.

By creating a cheese plate, you are taking time for both yourself and those around you. You're finding a sense of tranquility by taking pleasure in the present moment, and in the present cheese plate. You're expressing your creativity while bringing an intricate artwork to life. Sharing this moment with your guests is a fulfilling and valuable experience. It is the true essence of self-care. That Cheese Plate changed my life, and now I hope it can change yours.

acknowledgments

I want to thank my family, Ellen, Jim, and Shayne Mullen for the endless love and support. Countless holiday cheese plates led to the creation of this book. Clio Seraphim and Whitney Frick at the Dial Press and Eve Atterman at WME—That Cheese Team! Thank you for believing in this book and for being my cheerleaders along the way. To Sara Gilanchi, this book would be nothing without your incredible illustrations. The Cheese Party (you know who you are, from all the eras of my life)—thank you for being my best friends and soul family. I'm honored that we can always come together over a cheese plate. Jon Batiste and *The Late Show* team—thank you for supporting the cheese hustle while I still worked in the entertainment industry, shipping cheese tote bags from under my desk. Thank you to all of the incredible cheese makers and cheesemongers for teaching me everything I know about cheese. Last but definitely not least, thank you to all of the amazing people who follow @ThatCheesePlate and @CheeseByNumbers. You truly have made this possible and allowed That Cheese Plate to change my life.

Spread joy, stay positive, and always embrace your creativity.

Love,
Marissa

Thank you to the cheesemakers and brands involved in this book:

Ambrosi Cheese, Ardith Mae Farm, Beecher's Cheese, Bee Seasonal Honey, Boska Holland, Brooklyn Slate, Cabot Cheese, California Milk Advisory Board, Carnivore Club, Cato Corner Farm, CHEVOO, Clark Farms, Churchtown Dairy, Creminelli, Cypress Grove Creamery, Dalmatia Spreads, Dorothy Creamery, Edouard Massih, Effie's Homemade, Emmi Cheese, Essex Street Cheese, Firehook Crackers, Forever Cheese Co., French Cheese Corner, Hellenic Farms, Jammy Yummy, Jasper Hill Farm, La Quercia, Marieke Gouda, Mary's Gone Crackers, Mike's Hot Honey, Monty's NYC, Murray's Cheese, Nduja Artisans, Plymouth Cheese, Point Reyes Creamery, Quince and Apple, Roth Cheese, Rustic Bakery, Saxelby Cheesemongers, She Wolf Bakery, Treat Bakeshop, Union Square Greenmarket, Uplands Creamery, Vermont Creamery, Von Trapp Farmstead, Whole Foods Market, Windfall Farms, Wisconsin Cheese, and Z Crackers.

index

MARISSA MULLEN is a Brooklyn-based creative director, content creator, photographer, and food stylist. Previously hailing from a background in the music business and late-night television, Marissa followed her passion for cheese plates, which led her down a unique path. She is the founder of That Cheese Plate, a community for cheese lovers from across the globe, and Cheese By Numbers, the method behind crafting the perfect cheese plate.

Featured on the *Today* show, the *Rachael Ray Show, Live with Kelly and Ryan, Refinery29, Vox,* and *Food & Wine,* among many others, Marissa's cheese plates have inspired many. With her skillful abilities to curate experiences in both music and food, Marissa is dedicated to bringing people together through creativity, expression, and entertainment, an intention that is at the core of every pursuit.

@thatcheeseplate
@cheesebynumbers
thatcheeseplate.com
marissamullen.com

SARA GILANCHI is an illustrator, researcher, and aspiring dog owner living in Brooklyn. Her work has appeared in *The New Yorker*'s "Daily Shouts" and you can find more of it on Instagram (@saragilanchi) and at saragilanchi.com.